W9-BGR-841

Current
CONTROVERSIES

America's Mental Health Crisis

Other Books in the Current Controversies Series

America's Mental Health Crisis

Nadra Nittle, Book Editor

GREENHAVEN
PUBLISHING

Published in 2020 by Greenhaven Publishing, LLC
353 3rd Avenue, Suite 255, New York, NY 10010

Articles in Greenhaven Publishing anthologies are often edited for length to meet page
requirements. In addition, original titles of these works are changed to clearly present
the main thesis and to explicitly indicate the author's opinion. Every effort is made to
ensure that Greenhaven Publishing accurately reflects the original intent of the authors.
Every effort has been made to trace the owners of the copyrighted material.

Cover image: GrAl/Shutterstock.com

Library of Congress Cataloging-in-Publication Data

Names: Nittle, Nadra, editor.
Title: America's mental health crisis / Nadra Nittle, book editor.
Description: First edition. | New York : Greenhaven Publishing, 2020. | Series: Current
controversies | Includes bibliographical references and index. | Audience: Grades 9–12.
Identifiers: LCCN 2019022671 | ISBN 9781534506145 (library
binding) | ISBN 9781534506138 (paperback)
Subjects: LCSH: Mental health services—United States—Juvenile literature.
Classification: LCC RC454.4 .A45 2020 | DDC 362.20973—dc23
LC record available at https://lccn.loc.gov/2019022671

Manufactured in the United States of America

Website: http://greenhavenpublishing.com

Contents

Chapter 1: Do Aspects of Life in the United States Contribute to Mental Health Problems?

Temma Ehrenfeld

Tragically, suicides are on the rise in the US, but Americans of all ages are also more likely to get treatment for mental health care than they once were. There is no single cause for the rising number of mental health diagnoses, but a major factor is that mental illness is less stigmatized.

Yes: Life in the US Leads to Psychological Problems

Melanie Greenberg

People have always been social creatures, but in modern American society, problems such as loneliness and social isolation are daily realities. They're both sources of stress that can lead to serious health problems.

Monnica T. Williams

African Americans have historically faced racism and continue to experience discrimination today. The legacy of racism in the United States is so traumatizing for black people that it has long-lasting psychological effects on them, which often manifest as physical health problems as well.

The Pew Research Center

Fewer people than ever in the United States regularly attend worship services, but faith communities have long been places where Americans form social bonds, share problems, and receive prayer and counseling. Americans who attend worship services regularly are more likely than their nonreligious counterparts to say that they feel a sense of spiritual peace and well-being on a routine basis.

Chapter 2: Are People with Mental Illnesses Stigmatized in the United States?

individuals with mental health conditions lead quality lives, more needs to be learned about the relationship between stigma and mental illness.

Yes: Society Does Stigmatize People with Mental Illness

idea that mentally ill people are dangerous. It's important to challenge the media's depiction of mental disorders to prevent the public from falling for these misconceptions.

No: Society Does Not Stigmatize People with Mental Illness

Chapter 3: Are Barriers to Treatment a Problem in the United States?

Yes: Barriers to Treatment Are a Problem in the US

their needs. This has led to rural populations having worse mental health on average than the general US population.

In 2018, the actress Taraji P. Henson started a foundation to support mental health endeavors for black Americans and to destigmatize mental illnesses. This is just one part of a larger nationwide effort to promote greater accessibility to mental health care.

Chapter 4: Does Social Media Contribute to Americans' Mental Health Problems?

Jennifer Mattern

Social media is often held responsible for negatively influencing the mental health of users, especially teens and young adults. It can inhibit the growth of personal relationships, but social media has also been found to have a number of benefits. Many people with mental health disorders have used it to connect with others in their predicament.

Yes: Social Media Causes Mental Health Problems

Gigen Mammoser

Research has found a direct link between the amount of time a person spends on social media and one's level of personal contentment. Researchers concluded that people who spend less time on social media are happier and less lonely than their social media–hooked counterparts.

Hannah Blum

Social media can take a toll on one's mental health, especially during a breakup. The best move a person enduring a romantic split can make is to stay off social media, as it keeps users connected to the very people they need to distance themselves from most.

W. Keith Campbell

While narcissism existed long before the development of social media, social media encourages and rewards attention-seeking narcissistic behaviors, making it more socially acceptable than in the past. The exact relationship between social media and narcissism is hard to define, but it is clear that narcissistic behavior is more visible than ever as a result.

No: Social Media Does Not Cause Mental Health Problems

Foreword

"Controversy" is a word that has an undeniably unpleasant connotation. It carries a definite negative charge. Controversy can spoil family gatherings, spread a chill around classroom and campus discussion, inflame public discourse, open raw civic wounds, and lead to the ouster of public officials. We often feel that controversy is almost akin to bad manners, a rude and shocking eruption of that which must not be spoken or thought of in polite, tightly guarded society. To avoid controversy, to quell controversy, is often seen as a public good, a victory for etiquette, perhaps even a moral or ethical imperative.

Yet the studious, deliberate avoidance of controversy is also a whitewashing, a denial, a death threat to democracy. It is a false sterilizing and sanitizing and superficial ordering of the messy, ragged, chaotic, at times ugly processes by which a healthy democracy identifies and confronts challenges, engages in passionate debate about appropriate approaches and solutions, and arrives at something like a consensus and a broadly accepted and supported way forward. Controversy is the megaphone, the speaker's corner, the public square through which the citizenry finds and uses its voice. Controversy is the life's blood of our democracy and absolutely essential to the vibrant health of our society.

Our present age is certainly no stranger to controversy. We are consumed by fierce debates about technology, privacy, political correctness, poverty, violence, crime and policing, guns, immigration, civil and human rights, terrorism, militarism, environmental protection, and gender and racial equality. Loudly competing voices are raised every day, shouting opposing opinions, putting forth competing agendas, and summoning starkly different visions of a utopian or dystopian future. Often these voices attempt to shout the others down; there is precious little listening and considering among the cacophonous din. Yet listening and considering, too, are essential to the health of a democracy. If controversy is democracy's lusty lifeblood, respectful listening and careful thought are its higher faculties, its brain, its conscience.

Current Controversies does not shy away from or attempt to hush the loudly competing voices. It seeks to provide readers with as wide and representative as possible a range of articulate voices on any given controversy of the day, separates each one out to allow it to be heard clearly and fairly, and encourages careful listening to each of these well-crafted, thoughtfully expressed opinions, supplied by some of today's leading academics, thinkers, analysts, politicians, policy makers, economists, activists, change agents, and advocates. Only after listening to a wide range of opinions on an issue, evaluating the strengths and weaknesses of each argument, assessing how well the facts and available evidence mesh with the stated opinions and conclusions, and thoughtfully and critically examining one's own beliefs and conscience can the reader begin to arrive at his or her own conclusions and articulate his or her own stance on the spotlighted controversy.

This process is facilitated and supported in each Current Controversies volume by an introduction and chapter overviews that provide readers with the essential context they need to begin engaging with the spotlighted controversies, with the debates surrounding them, and with their own perhaps shifting or nascent opinions on them. Chapters are organized around several key questions that are answered with diverse opinions representing all points on the political spectrum. In its content, organization, and methodology, readers are encouraged to determine the authors' point of view and purpose, interrogate and analyze the various arguments and their rhetoric and structure, evaluate the arguments' strengths and weaknesses, test their claims against available facts and evidence, judge the validity of the reasoning, and bring into clearer, sharper focus the reader's own beliefs and conclusions and how they may differ from or align with those in the collection or those of classmates.

Research has shown that reading comprehension skills improve dramatically when students are provided with compelling, intriguing, and relevant "discussable" texts. The subject matter of these collections could not be more compelling, intriguing, or urgently relevant to today's students and the world they are poised to inherit. The anthologized articles also provide the basis for stimulating, lively, and passionate classroom debates. Students who are compelled to anticipate objections to their own argument and identify the flaws in those of an opponent read more carefully, think more critically, and steep themselves in relevant context, facts, and information more thoroughly. In short, using discussable text of the kind provided by every single volume in the Current Controversies series encourages close reading, facilitates reading comprehension, fosters research, strengthens critical thinking, and greatly enlivens and energizes classroom discussion and participation. The entire learning process is deepened, extended, and strengthened.

If we are to foster a knowledgeable, responsible, active, and engaged citizenry, we must provide readers with the intellectual, interpretive, and critical-thinking tools and experience necessary to make sense of the world around them and of the all-important debates and arguments that inform it. We must encourage them not to run away from or attempt to quell controversy but to embrace it in a responsible, conscientious, and thoughtful way, to sharpen and strengthen their own informed opinions by listening to and critically analyzing those of others. This series encourages respectful engagement with and analysis of current controversies and competing opinions and fosters a resulting increase in the strength and rigor of one's own opinions and stances. As such, it helps readers assume their rightful place in the public square and provides them with the skills necessary to uphold their awesome responsibility—guaranteeing the continued and future health of a vital, vibrant, and free democracy.

Introduction

> *"It's time to tell everyone who's dealing*
> *with a mental health issue that*
> *they're not alone."*
> *-Michelle Obama, "Change*
> *Direction" speech, March 4, 2015.*

More Americans than ever say they're facing psychological distress. A variety of studies have found that the number of people nationally seeking therapy, medication, and other services for mental illness is climbing. According to an analysis of a federal health survey of more than 140,000 adults in the United States, the percentage of Americans receiving mental health care grew from 19 to 23 percent between 2004 and 2015[1]. These individuals aren't keeping quiet about their diagnoses, either.

Celebrities such as Ariana Grande, Selena Gomez, Mariah Carey, and Pete Davidson have all opened up about their struggles with mental illness. The same goes for social media users who include hashtags like #TherapyHelped in posts about the benefits of mental health care. Young adults in particular aren't shy about sharing their mental health struggles. This is a large reason why colleges and universities have seen a boost in students seeking counseling on campus.

That more Americans of all ages are turning to mental health care has generated not only praise but fear as well. Why do conditions like depression and anxiety appear to be on the rise? It's tempting to point the finger at the nation's shifting culture. A growing number of Americans are socially isolated; they live alone and aren't a part of organized communities, spiritual or otherwise. They may not even leave home to work or shop. Loneliness certainly raises the odds of developing mental illness, but staying in an unhealthy relationship to avoid singleness is equally troubling.

Social isolation is just one of many risk factors for mental illness. Financial problems play a role as well. A decade after the US economy spiraled into the Great Recession of 2007–2009, some Americans have yet to fully recover from the financial crisis. Analysts say the recession led to the so-called "gig economy" that saw a rise in freelance and part-time work. In 2019, *Business Insider* reported that there were 40 percent—or 1.4 million—more Americans working in part-time jobs because they couldn't find full-time work than there had been a decade earlier.[2] This trend has made it difficult for young adults to find stable employment, become financially secure, or buy homes. The gig economy has also resulted in a "burnout" culture in which exploited workers take on more tasks than they can handle. They go without sleep, neglect their friends and families, and give up their leisure time— all to be more productive. Before long, overworking takes a toll on them and they feel too burned out to perform their job duties or anything else. Burnout leads to stress, sadness, and fatigue, but burnout culture is growing in an economy in which workers have fewer employment options than they had just ten years ago.

As some Americans toil away in exploitative jobs, they log onto social media websites and see their old classmates leading "perfect" lives. This is a uniquely twenty-first century trend, and scholars have linked social media use to depression. Users who don't feel like they measure up to others often feel badly about themselves. But some researchers say social media has been unfairly blamed for mental health problems. After all, people have always compared themselves to others. Social media just makes it more convenient to compare.

If the country's mental health crisis can't be blamed on a particular aspect of modern life—be it social media or the economy—then what's responsible? One could argue that Americans today aren't any worse off psychologically than they were a century or more ago. Mental illness, after all, has been a part of the human experience for millennia. It is even described in ancient texts such as the Bible. Today, we simply have names for mental health problems—from depression to narcissism to schizophrenia. We also have formal ways of treating these conditions. Advances in psychology and decreased stigmatization of mental illnesses have increasingly led Americans to get treatment. More than any other factor, the uptick in mental health diagnoses may be attributed to the rising numbers of people getting mental healthcare services.[3]

As more people seek help, challenges in mental healthcare remain. In immigrant communities or communities of color, going to therapy or taking medication for a mental health condition may still be regarded as taboo. In others, especially rural communities, a lack of treatment providers makes it difficult to get any form of care. Nationwide, insurance companies make it challenging for patients to access a variety of treatment options. They may only cover a limited amount of therapy sessions or make it difficult for patients to see therapists who are out of network, not to mention that many therapists don't take insurance at all.

Current Controversies: America's Mental Health Crisis will investigate the ongoing debates about mental illness in the United States. An eclectic mix of bloggers, patients, and experts explore how mental health and societal trends intersect. Are more Americans than ever mentally ill, or are more Americans just getting the help they need? By reviewing opposing perspectives, readers reflect on the basis for each argument before forming their own unique opinion on mental health in America.

Notes

1. Dennis Thompson, "More Are Seeking Mental Health Care, But Not Always Those Who Need It Most," USNews.com, Dec. 7, 2018. http://www.usnews.com/news /health-news/articles/2018-12-07/more-are-seeking-mental-health-care-but-not -always-those-who-need-it-most.

2. Jim Edwards, "Unemployment Is Low Only Because 'Involuntary' Part-Time Work Is High," *Business Insider*, January 27, 2019. http://www.businessinsider.com /unemployment-vs-involuntary-part-time-work-underemployment-2019-1.

3. Dennis Thompson, "More Are Seeking Mental Health Care, but Not Always Those Who Need It Most," USNews.com, Dec. 7, 2018. http://www.usnews.com/news /health-news/articles/2018-12-07/more-are-seeking-mental-health-care-but-not -always-those-who-need-it-most.

Do Aspects of Life in the United States Contribute to Mental Health Problems?

Americans Have Mental Health Problems for a Wide Range of Reasons

Temma Ehrenfeld

Temma Ehrenfeld is a New York-based writer, editor, and blogger who covers psychology, health, and personal finance.

It's hard to miss, with rising rates of suicide and depression: American mental health seems to be in a downturn.

Days after the suicide of fashion designer Kate Spade, at 55, the Centers for Disease Control and Prevention (CDC) reported that suicides are becoming more common in every age group, but especially in mid-life.

The biggest increase was among men ages 45 to 64, and suicide is rising among mid-life women, too.

Young people—from teens to college students—are another group that appears to be greatly affected by the mental health storm that's growing in America.

In the last decade, Lisa Cohen, PhD, clinical professor of psychiatry at Mount Sinai Beth Israel in New York, has seen a bump in college students and young adults from stable families landing in the hospital at risk for suicide after a minor stress.

In part, that may be because they've been overprotected—but the overall ramp up in stress during early adulthood is also steeper today than it's been in the past.

"While earlier generations could rely on a steady supply of jobs in large, stable companies, this is no longer the case," Cohen says. "Many young people expect to work in start-ups or to work freelance . . . [They] look ahead to an economic life of uncertainty, without a clear path to success or even self-sufficiency."

At the same time, they face heavy college loans and a technology-dominated social world that requires a thicker skin.

"Depression: The Growing American Mental Health Storm," by Temma Ehrenfeld, Healthline Media, July 31, 2018. Reprinted by permission.

The less secure economy and less social contact may be at work in mid-life despair as well.

Prompt treatment for depression is important to overall health. Untreated depression raises the risk of stroke, heart attacks, dementia, and Parkinson's—especially in older people.

And once a person is ill, depression can make recovery more difficult.

More Depressed Young

Some of the rise in rates of depression might be attributed to more people seeking care as mental illness becomes less stigmatized. However, the recent bumps in numbers of depressed people have happened too quickly to entirely fit that explanation.

For example, diagnoses of major depression rose by a third between 2013 and 2016, in a report analyzing claims to Blue Cross Blue Shield Association.

This data revealed increases in all age groups for both men and women—but particular spikes among teens and young adults through age 35.

In research based on national surveys including the uninsured, more than 11 percent of teens, and 9.6 percent of Americans ages 18 to 25, had major depression in the most recent year.

Thoughts of suicide have also been found to be common among teens, though much smaller numbers take action.

More than 22 percent of American high school girls think about attempting suicide, according to 2013 CDC data. Of that group, 3.6 percent took steps that resulted in an injury, poisoning, or overdose that required medical care.

The numbers were roughly half for boys: Nearly 12 percent considered suicide and less than 2 percent took actions that required medical care.

In surveys that ask teens and college students whether they engage in self-hurting behavior such as cutting or burning their skin, as many as 40 percent say yes, though it's not clear whether those figures are rising.

Self-hurting behavior is a risk factor for suicide attempts.

"When I started in the field in the late 1980s, young patients with severe suicidal ideation or self-injurious behavior, like cutting, came from very disturbed backgrounds and often had histories of considerable trauma," Cohen says.

Today, they may be from stable, supportive families.

The Case Against Smartphones

Why now? One big obvious change is the rise of social media and the smartphone.

Based on two large US surveys of 8th- through 12th-graders, researchers argued that screen time tracked closely with reported mental health issues.

This was true for individual kids—the more time on the phone, the more likely they were to report symptoms of depression. It was also true for the numbers as a whole, lead author, San Diego State University psychologist Jean Twenge, PhD, reported.

Kids began getting smartphones between 2010 and 2015. As the phones spread, overall depression symptoms increased, year by year, she said.

In the same period, visits to counseling centers at colleges jumped 30 percent.

A social media habit has also been tied to depression in studies of 19- to 32-year-olds, though it may matter most how often they look.

Today, for people in their 20s and 30s, technology dominates dating.

New apps put an unprecedented number of choices at their fingertips—but that's also made many feel more hopeless about finding love, says Loren Soeiro, PhD, a clinical psychologist in New York.

"I talk to a lot of people about how these dating apps make them feel. They feel commodified and given a very small chance," he says.

For those who are vulnerable to feeling left out, social media shows them acquaintances having more fun than they are. And for those who try to compete, the competition can be constant.

"There is no privacy," Cohen points out, adding there's also a constant pressure to impress. "With social media people are meaner to each other, continually marketing themselves, and unable to escape the intrusive public eye."

Playing on smartphones can often cut into sleep as well. Some 60 percent of teens spend the last hour of the day with their phone—and end up losing an hour of sleep compared to peers who do something else at bedtime.

A teen who gets six hours or less of sleep triples their chance of becoming depressed.

Growing Loneliness

Other research found that loneliness is at "epidemic levels" in the United States.

In a May report from Cigna, only around half of Americans said they have daily meaningful in-person conversations with a friend or family member. Most Americans qualify as "lonely."

For example, when asked how often they feel that no one knows them well, 54 percent said they feel that way always or sometimes.

Generation Z—adults between the ages of 18 and 22—emerged as the loneliest, regardless of how much time they spent online or on their phones.

Living Single

More adults—42 percent—live without a spouse or romantic partner, a number that has grown since 2007 in all age groups under 65.

That number is even higher for those aged 18 to 35. About 61 percent live as singletons—up from 56 percent in 2007.

It's not clear that married people are happier, healthier, or are less lonely—yet many unpartnered people assume they are and feel left out.

It *is* clear that living single is tied to less financial security, a Pew Research Center report notes.

More than half of working-age adults without a job were living single in 2017, sharply up from a decade earlier. They don't have access to a spouse's health insurance or cushion when their income falls.

Mid-Life Despair

For decades, suicide rates had been falling. However, in the new CDC suicide data, the average yearly growth rate doubled beginning in 2006 to 2 percent a year.

Most Americans who die of suicide are white, working-class, middle-aged men.

About 20 veterans also die of suicide each day, most of them over the age of 50.

Men are more likely to use guns than women and less likely to seek help. But with rates rising among women, the gap has narrowed.

Pooling together the sexes, the rate of suicide in the 45-to-64 age group rose 45 percent from 2000 to 2016.

Suicides tend to increase during recessions, and the most recent one "may have left the middle-aged population especially hard hit," suggested Anne Schuchat, principal deputy director at the CDC.

Job prospects for men without a college degree have been dwindling for some time, and they're now more likely than before to be single.

Beyond the suicide numbers, some take the "slow suicide" route and die of drug overdoses or alcohol liver disease.

What You Can Do

Although depression can make it much harder, *now* is the time to take good care of yourself.

If you or someone you know is struggling with depression, be persistent about finding the right medical care—ideally both medication and counseling—and use that boost to focus on good health habits across life.

Exercise helps, though research suggests it won't substitute for therapy. Mind your diet and sleep, as well as hygiene, and cultivate in-person social ties.

For parents, the tendency is to worry most about teens who are acting out. But, according to a 2014 study of more than 12,000 European teens, an "invisible risk group" of teens don't exercise, skip sleep, and spend a lot of time online.

More than 13 percent were depressed and nearly 6 percent attempted suicide.

Parents can promote in-person social activities for children to help them fight the trend of spending hours alone in their room and limit screen time by barring phones and laptops from beds.

Loss of appetite emerged as a red flag for suicidal thinking in a study in Japan of more than 18,000 teens.

What your child eats matters, too. Skipping vegetables and fruits and sticking to foods like meat and bread is depressing, according to research with more than 7,000 teens.

Don't wait more than a year to get help for a child with suicidal thinking: Research suggests that treatment within the first 6 to 12 months after the suicidal thoughts begin is most effective.

Should your teen take an antidepressant? The usual recommendation is a combination of talk therapy and antidepressants, although a 2014 review from the prestigious Cochrane Review concluded that this approach remains unproven.

No teen should have access to guns, alcohol, painkillers, or sleeping pills at home. Don't assume you'll see the red flags in time to whisk the pills away.

Young people sometimes act on a suicidal impulse within minutes or a day.

Loneliness Is a Dangerous Source of Stress for Americans Today

Melanie Greenberg

Melanie Greenberg is a psychologist with more than twenty years of experience as a clinician, professor, and researcher. She is the author of The Stress-Proof Brain, *published in 2017.*

Feeling lonely is stressful for your mind and body. Our ancestors lived in tribes and relied on others to hunt or gather food, raise their young, and fight off predators. Your brain is wired to connect with other people, and it interprets loneliness as a chronic stressor, triggering your "fight, flight, or freeze" response. Over time, chronic exposure to stress hormones like cortisol can damage your health.

In research, loneliness and lack of social and community ties has been linked to inflammation, gene expression, and even higher mortality rates. Therefore, it's important to recognize when you are lonely and to take steps to engage more deeply with other people.

How Do I Know If I Am Too Lonely?

There are two kinds of loneliness. The first is *social isolation*. You may spend a lot of time alone, without a solid network of friends and family to hang out with. The second type of loneliness is *feeling lonely*. You can be lonely even in a crowded room if you don't feel cared about or feel like your needs are important to others. You may have friends, coworkers, or family, but not feel that they can be relied on for emotional or practical support. The two don't always overlap. You can live alone yet not feel lonely, because you do lots of fun, social activities. And you can feel lonely even though you're married, because you and your spouse lead separate lives.

"Feeling Lonely? You May Be Damaging Your Health," by Melanie Greenberg Ph.D., *Psychology Today*, Sussex Publishers, LLC, September 19, 2017. Reprinted by permission.

What Are the Causes of Loneliness?

Some loneliness may be inevitable as you age: Friends die or move away, or family members are too busy juggling work and kids to visit or call. You may be more lonely at certain stages of your life, such as when you start college, after you graduate, when you have a new baby, after relocating, after your kids leave home, or after you retire or lose your spouse. Today, many parents shape their lives around their kids' activities, with little time to deepen and invest in their own friendships, resulting in loneliness when their kids move away. But loneliness can also be a subjective feeling unrelated to any particular life stage.

What Is the Effect of Loneliness on Health?

Both social isolation and feeling lonely seem to be bad for your health, but feeling lonely may be worse. Using tools from molecular biology, researchers have been studying the effects of loneliness on people's genes. They've found that genes that promote inflammation are more active in lonely people; in addition, genes that inhibit inflammation are less active in lonely people. This may explain why loneliness increases your risk for inflammatory conditions such as asthma and autoimmune diseases. It has also been well-established that loneliness is a significant risk factor for earlier mortality; its effects on health are the same or greater than obesity or smoking. Therefore, it is important to take steps to try to reduce loneliness if you can. And on a societal level, we need to provide more opportunities for lonely people to socialize, particularly when they are elderly.

Assessing Your Loneliness

Researchers assess loneliness with statements like the following. These represent just a sample of items, and is not a validated questionnaire, so it can't tell you whether you are lonelier than is healthy. But it can give you an indication of an area of your life that may need improving.

Tally all of the statements below that are true for you:

- I don't have people to hang out with or do things with.
- When I need help, there's nobody to ask.
- I don't have close friends.
- I don't feel part of a group or community.
- I don't have anyone to talk to.
- My relationships are superficial.

If you counted more than half the items, you should consider whether loneliness may be a chronic stressor for you.

What Can I Do to Prevent Loneliness?

Develop a Few Close, Caring Relationships with Friends, Family, or Coworkers

Put effort into maintaining your closest relationships by checking in regularly, acknowledging important life events, listening, showing up when they need you, and being there through life's ups and downs.

Get Out More

Think about group sporting, creative, social, or volunteer activities that you would naturally enjoy or find meaningful. Do some research and make a specific plan about how to fit these into your busy schedule. What are you willing to let go of to make more time for socializing?

Take Inventory of Your Relationships

If most of your relationships are superficial, consider if you'd like to go deeper with these people. Are they capable of being the kind of close friend you'd like? Depending on the answer, you may decide to speak up more about your needs, reach out and initiate more, or look for different types of friends.

Have Patience with New Relationships

Don't expect too much at the beginning. Friendships take time to build naturally. Try not to be too demanding of a new friend's time, and don't take it personally if they say "no" to an arrangement. They may already have a full life and will make more space for you over time.

Be Proactive in Organizing Activities

Organize a potluck party for coworkers or neighbors. Talk to your acquaintances about starting a book club or clothing swap. Start a regular dog-walking group. Organize a weekend outing or a picnic. It takes courage and lots of effort to be a social organizer, but the rewards should be well worth it.

Feeling lonely is a sign that your relationships or community ties are not meeting your social or emotional needs. It's easy to feel like a victim when you're lonely, but that won't help. Try to see your loneliness as situational or due to a lack of effort, rather than a sign of innate personal inadequacy. Some people are lucky enough to be born into families with lots of connections, while others have to build social networks for themselves. For most of us, loneliness is a challenge that you can conquer with some investment of time, effort, and emotional energy.

Racism and Psychological Distress Go Hand in Hand

Monnica T. Williams

Dr. Monnica T. Williams is a clinical psychologist and associate professor in the department of psychological sciences at the University of Connecticut. She also serves as director of the university's Laboratory for Culture and Mental Health Disparities and as clinical director of the Behavioral Wellness Clinic in Tolland, Connecticut.

Post-traumatic stress disorder (PTSD)—the diagnosis conjures up images of hollow-eyed combat veterans or terrified rape victims, but new research indicates that racism can be just as devastating as gunfire or sexual assault. In a previous article I posed the question, Can Racism Cause PTSD? The answer is yes, and changes in the DSM-5 open the door for a better understanding of this phenomenon. Here I discuss the psychological research in this area, as well as clinical observations and how these relate to my own experiences as a person of color. Several people have asked me why I focus on African Americans, given the many similar experiences faced by other ethnic/racial groups, immigrants, sexual minorities, disabled people, and other stigmatized individuals. I want to state up front that the problems faced by those groups are real and deserve attention too, however in this article I am going to stick to what I know, the Black experience in America.

Racism-related experiences can range from frequent ambiguous "microaggressions" to blatant hate crimes and physical assault. Racial microaggressions are subtle, yet pervasive acts of racism; these can be brief remarks, vague insults, or even non-verbal exchanges, such as a scowl or refusal to sit next to a Black person on the subway. When experiencing microaggressions, the target loses vital mental resources trying figure out the intention of one

"The Link Between Racism and PTSD," by Monnica T Williams Ph.D., *Psychology Today*, Sussex Publishers, LLC, September 6, 2015. Reprinted by permission.

committing the act. These events may happen frequently, making it difficult to mentally manage the sheer volume of racial stressors. The unpredictable and anxiety-provoking nature of the events, which may be dismissed by others, can lead to victims feeling as if they are "going crazy." Chronic fear of these experiences may lead to constant vigilance or even paranoia, which over time may result in traumatization or contribute to PTSD when a more stressful event occurs later. In fact, one study of female veterans found that African Americans scored higher on measures of ideas of persecution and paranoia, which the authors attributed to an adaptive response to racism.

While most of us can understand why a violent hate crime could be traumatizing, the traumatizing role of microaggressions can be difficult to comprehend, especially among those who do not experience them. One study of racial discrimination and psychopathology across three US ethnic minority groups found that African Americans experienced significantly more instances of discrimination than either Asian or Hispanic Americans. Non-Hispanic Whites experience the least discrimination (11% for Whites versus 81% for Blacks). Furthermore, those African Americans who experienced the most racism were significantly more likely to experience symptoms of PTSD as well.

Make no mistake, Asian and Hispanic Americans receive their unfair share of racism too, and research shows that it may even be harder to manage for individuals in these groups. But each ethnic/racial group has its own package of negative stereotypes that impact the form of racism experienced, so it's not surprising that PTSD prevalence differs by race and ethnicity. Findings from large-scale national studies indicate that, while African Americans have a lower risk for many anxiety disorders, they have a 9.1% prevalence rate for PTSD, compared to 6.8% in Whites. That means that almost one in ten Black people becomes traumatized, and I think these rates may actually be higher since diagnosticians are usually not considering the role of racism in causing trauma. Studies also show that African Americans with PTSD experience significantly more impairment due to trauma, indicating greater difficulty carrying out daily activities and increased barriers to receiving effective treatment.

Research has linked racism to a host of other problems, including serious psychological distress, physical health problems, depression, anxiety, binge drinking, and even disordered eating. A strong, positive African American identity can be a potential protective factor against symptoms of anxiety and depression, but this is not adequate protection when the discriminatory events are severe.

I have spoken to African Americans all over the country about their experiences with race-based stress and trauma. One veteran in Colorado told me about how the bullets he faced in combat were nothing compared to the mistreatment he experienced at the hands of his fellow soldiers in arms. When he searched for treatment for his resulting mental health issues, the VA system could not find a qualified therapist to help him. I recently assessed a woman for whom the racial climate at work became so oppressive that she was no longer able to function at her job. She tearfully described the ongoing racial-harassment she experienced from her supervisor, while co-workers turned a blind eye. She carried a stack of documents to prove everything that had happened to her because she didn't think anyone would believe it. My heart breaks because I have heard her story in many forms, more than once.

It's important to understand that race-based stress and trauma extends beyond the direct behaviors of prejudiced individuals. We are surrounded by constant reminders that race-related danger can occur at any time, anywhere, to anyone. We might see clips on the nightly news featuring unarmed African Americans being killed on the street, in a holding cell, or even in a church. Learning of these events brings up an array of painful racially-charged memories, and what has been termed "vicarious traumatization." Even if the specific tragic news item has never happened to us directly, we may have had parents or aunts who have had similar experiences, or we know people in our community who have, and their stories have been passed down. Over the centuries the Black community has developed a cultural knowledge of these sorts of horrific events, which then primes us for traumatization when we hear about yet another act of violence. Another unarmed Black man has been shot by police in our communities and nowhere feels safe.

Research shows that trauma can alter one's perceptions of overall safety in society. Black people with PTSD have been found to have lower expectations about the benevolence of the world than Whites. When comparing Black and White Americans, one study reported that African Americans held more negative perceptions of the world, appearing more skeptical and mistrustful. Experiencing a traumatic event changed perceptions of the world in White victims from positive to negative, yet the perceptions of Black victims were not impacted by traumatic experiences. My take on this is that they are already traumatized by life in America. Most of us with dark skin know the world is not safe.

Once sensitized through ongoing racism, routine slights may take an increasingly greater toll. Microaggressions, such as being followed by security guards in a department store, or seeing a White woman clutching her purse in an elevator when a Black man enters, is just another trigger for racial stress. Social messages and stereotypes may blame the victim, and tell us that Blacks need to stop "dressing like thugs," "get off welfare," and assimilate into White culture to gain acceptance. But these experiences can happen to any Black person of any social status. Sometimes higher status Black people experience more discrimination because they threaten the social order and thus draw increased hate from others. I've experienced this myself on plenty of occasions. For example once when I was working as a psychological intern in a metropolitan hospital, I was followed by security guards to my car after work. Apparently, a co-worker was frightened by me simply because I was Black. It did not matter that I was a qualified medical professional engaged in patient care and with no history of violence. I remember feeling helpless, angry, and confused. I went over the experience in my mind repeatedly, and tried to figure out who had made the call and why. Victims often feel powerless to stop these experiences because the discrimination is so persistent. Those who are exposed to this type of racial oppression may turn their frustration inward, resulting in depression and disability, or respond outwardly through aggression or violence.

I often wonder how people can continue to remain resilient in the face of ongoing, undeserved discrimination. Within the Black community, positive coping with racism may involve faith, forgiveness, humor, and optimism. These cultural values have allowed African Americans to persevere for centuries even under the most oppressive conditions. One area we are currently studying in my research lab is how African Americans can proactively cope with racism. We are also developing treatments for race-based stress and trauma to enable those who are suffering to move beyond their painful experiences and become stronger, so they can re-engage in larger society. But patching up injured victims of racism one-by-one only goes so far. I don't think it is reasonable to expect that we can "fix" people to enable them to manage constant, ongoing acts of prejudice with a smile, and ask them to be perpetually polite, productive, and forgiving. What we really need is a large-scale shift in our social consciousness to understand the toll this takes on the psyche of victims so that even small acts of racism become unacceptable. We need those who witness racism to speak out and victims to be believed.

Fewer Americans Rely on Faith Communities to Be Their Support Systems

The Pew Research Center

The Pew Research Center is a think tank that investigates national and global trends. It carries out demographic research, opinion polls, and analyses.

In recent years, the percentage of US adults who say they regularly attend religious services has been declining, while the share of Americans who attend only a few times a year, seldom or never has been growing. A new Pew Research Center survey finds that the main reason people regularly go to church, synagogue, mosque or another house of worship is an obvious one: to feel closer to God. But the things that keep people away from religious services are more complicated.

Among those who attend no more than a few times a year, about three-in-ten say they do not go to religious services for a simple reason: They are not believers. But a much larger share stay away *not* because of a lack of faith, but for other reasons. This includes many people who say one very important reason they don't regularly attend church is that they practice their faith in other ways. Others cite things they dislike about particular congregations or religious services (for example, they haven't found a church or house of worship they like, or they don't like the sermons). Still others name logistical reasons, like being in poor health or not having the time to go, as very important reasons for not regularly attending religious services.

By their own description, those who cite reasons *other* than a lack of belief for avoiding church are a fairly religious group. About

"Why Americans Go (and Don't Go) to Religious Services," Pew Research Center, Washington, DC (August 1, 2018). https://www.pewforum.org/2018/08/01/why-americans-go-to-religious-services/. Used in accordance with Pew Research Center reuse Policy. http://www.pewresearch.org/terms-and-conditions/. Usage in no way implies endorsement.

seven-in-ten identify with a religion (including six-in-ten who are Christian), and most say religion is either "very" or "somewhat" important in their lives. To be sure, they are not as religious as Americans who report going regularly to religious services. But by several standard measures, they are much more religious than those who say, "I am not a believer."

Demographically, more than half of those who do not attend church or another house of worship for reasons other than nonbelief are women, and they tend to be older, less highly educated and less Democratic compared with those who do not go because of a lack of faith. Meanwhile, those who refrain from attending religious services because they are nonbelievers are more highly educated and largely male, young and Democratic.

The new survey, conducted online Dec. 4 to 18, 2017, among a nationally representative sample of 4,729 adults on Pew Research Center's American Trends Panel, asked respondents who attend religious services a few times a year or less often (including those who never attend) whether each of eight reasons is "very important, somewhat important, or not important" for why they do not go to religious services more often.[1]

Overall, the single most common answer cited for not attending religious services is "I practice my faith in other ways," which is offered as a very important reason by 37% of people who rarely or never attend religious services. A similar share mention things they dislike about religious services or particular congregations, including one-in-four who say they have not yet found a house of worship they like, one-in-five who say they dislike the sermons, and 14% who say they do not feel welcome at religious services.

About three-in-ten non-attenders say they are not believers, while 22% cite logistical reasons for not going to religious services, such as not having the time or being in poor health. And fully a quarter of those who infrequently attend religious services say none of these factors is a very important reason why.

The survey also asked US adults who say they attend religious services at least once or twice per month about 10 possible reasons they may do so. In response, eight-in-ten regular attenders say becoming "closer to God" is a very important reason they go to religious services.[2]

Additionally, roughly two-thirds say they attend religious services to give their children a moral foundation, to become better people, and for comfort in times of trouble or sorrow. Smaller majorities say that valuable sermons and being part of "a community of faith" are very important reasons for their regular religious attendance.

Far fewer cite their family's religious traditions (37%) or a feeling of religious obligation (31%) as reasons for their steady religious attendance, while even fewer say socializing and meeting new people (19%) or pleasing their spouse or family (16%) are key reasons they attend church regularly.

In a follow-up question, regular worship attenders were asked to choose the *most* important reason they attend religious services.[3] Overall, six-in-ten indicate they go to religious services primarily to become closer to God, and no other reason comes close.[4] For example, just 8% say they go to religious services mainly to become a better person, and about one-in-twenty say they attend religious services primarily to be part of a community of faith, to find comfort in troubling times, to provide their children with a moral foundation, or because they find the sermons valuable.

Other findings from the new survey include:

- Eight-in-ten regular attenders say they "always" or "often" experience a sense of God's presence when they attend worship services. Nearly three-quarters say they "always" or "often" feel a sense of community with people who share their religion when they attend religious services, and six-in-ten say they feel a sense of connection to a longstanding tradition.
- Catholics who attend Mass regularly are significantly less likely than other Christian churchgoers to say that the sermons they hear are what keeps them coming back. Indeed, among those who attend church regularly, Protestants are

roughly twice as likely as Catholics (71% vs. 36%) to say valuable sermons are a very important reason.

- While the survey does not include measures of every conceivable way in which a person might put their religious convictions into practice (e.g., through environmental stewardship, social justice activism, etc.), those who avoid religious services because they "practice their faith in other ways" are *less* involved in a variety of community, charitable and social groups than are those who attend religious services regularly. Among those who cite practicing their faith in other ways as a very important reason for not attending religious services, 50% say they are active in at least one of several types of such groups measured by the survey, compared with 63% among regular attenders. And the people who say they practice their faith in other ways are far less religious, by a variety of traditional measures beyond worship attendance (including frequency of prayer, assessment of religion's importance in one's life, etc.), than those who attend religious services regularly.

- One-in-four respondents who rarely or never attend religious services (26%) give no specific reason why—they do not select any of the eight factors mentioned in the survey as very important reasons for not going to church. This group is considerably *more* religious than those who say they do not attend religious services because of a lack of faith, but somewhat *less* religious than those who cite other reasons (e.g., logistical difficulties or that they "practice their faith in other ways") for not going to church.

More than Four-in-Ten Christians Who Do Not Attend Religious Services Say They Practice Their Faith in Other Ways

Among self-identified Christians, the predominant reason that non-churchgoers offer for not attending worship services is that they practice their faith in other ways. Upwards of four-in-ten

(44%) say this is a very important reason for not going to church more often. The next most common reason Christians give for not attending services is that they haven't found a church or house of worship they like (28%).

By contrast, the most common reason religiously unaffiliated non-attenders do not attend religious services is a lack of belief (46% say this is a very important reason they do not attend religious services), while one-quarter cite practicing their faith in other ways as a central reason for not going to services.

Among both of these groups of non-attenders (self-identified Christians and religious "nones"), fewer cite not feeling welcome, not having time, being in poor health and not having a nearby house of worship for their religion or denomination as very important reasons for not going to services.

Women, adults ages 50 and older and those who identify as Republicans or lean toward the Republican Party are more likely than other groups of infrequent churchgoers to say they don't attend religious services because they practice their faith in other ways. Meanwhile, men, younger adults, college graduates and Democrats are more likely to cite a lack of belief as a very important reason they do not go to religious services.

The survey does not find much variation by race on these questions, although black respondents who do not attend church regularly are more likely than whites to say they do not go to church because they don't feel welcome and because there is no church for their religion nearby.

Religious and Demographic Profiles of Non-Attenders

The survey also makes it possible to flip the lens and analyze the data from the other direction—to ask, for example, who are the people who do not attend church because they simply do not believe in God or religion, and how do they compare with the people who do not attend church because they practice their faith in other ways or because they do not feel welcome?[5]

Most non-attenders who cite a lack of belief as a very important reason for not attending religious services are, simply put, not very religious. But those who cite other reasons as key explanations for not attending church are, overall, more religiously observant.

For instance, two-thirds of people who cite logistical reasons or that they "practice their faith in other ways" as very important factors in keeping them away from religious services identify with a religion (primarily Christianity), as do 56% of those who dislike features of particular congregations or religious services. Roughly half of those who say they practice their faith in other ways also report praying every day, as do 44% of those who name logistical reasons as key factors in keeping them away from church and 36% of those who dislike elements of services and congregations. By contrast, just 15% of those who do not attend religious services due to a lack of belief say they pray daily.

People who rarely or never attend religious services are younger, on average, than those who attend more regularly. And those who say they do not attend religious services because they don't have time are younger than other non-attenders. About seven-in-ten are under the age of 30, while one-in-five (22%) are between the ages of 50 and 64, and just 7% are over the age of 65. By contrast, those who do not attend religious services because they are in poor health are older than many other groups, with six-in-ten over the age of 50, and they also have less education than most other groups.

Democrats are less likely than Republicans to attend worship services regularly, and among non-attenders, those who say they eschew religious services because they are nonbelievers largely identify with or lean toward the Democratic Party—75%, vs. 22% who are Republicans. Republicans are more heavily concentrated, though still outnumbered, among those who say they don't attend for other reasons.

Across All Religious Groups, Large Majorities Cite Desire to Grow Closer to God as Key Reason for Attending Religious Services

Among those who attend religious services regularly, large majorities across all demographic groups and major Christian traditions say becoming "closer to God" is a very important factor in their decision to attend religious services. Smaller majorities in most Christian traditions name instilling a moral foundation in their children, becoming a better person, seeking comfort in times of trouble, finding value in the sermons, and being part of a community of faith as key reasons they attend religious services. Catholics are the only group of Christians in which fewer than half of regular churchgoers mention an appreciation of sermons as a key factor for why they go to Mass regularly.

In general, women are more likely than men to say that a variety of factors are very important for why they attend religious services regularly. There is one notable exception to this pattern—men are significantly more likely than women to say pleasing a spouse or other family member is a very important reason they go to religious services (22% vs. 12%).

Young adults who attend religious services regularly are more likely than older adults to do so for social reasons: 30% of adults under 30 say meeting new people or socializing is a key factor in why they attend religious services, compared with 19% or fewer among older age groups.

Black Americans who attend church regularly are more likely than their white or Hispanic counterparts to say becoming closer to God, becoming a better person, finding comfort in times of trouble or sorrow, finding the sermons valuable, and feeling a religious obligation are very important reasons for going to church.

At Religious Services, Eight-in-Ten Christians Regularly Feel a Sense of God's Presence

Majorities of US churchgoers say that when they're at religious services, they "always" or "often" feel a sense of God's presence

(80%), a sense of community with others (73%) and a sense of connection to a longstanding tradition (60%). Women are more likely than men to say they often or always have these feelings.

Adults under the age of 30 are about as likely as their older counterparts to say they feel a sense of connection to tradition or a sense of community while at religious services. But when it comes to feeling a sense of God's presence at services, younger adults are much less likely than their elders to say they experience this. Roughly six-in-ten adults under 30 (63%) often feel a sense of God's presence at religious services, compared with eight-in-ten or more in older age groups.

Notes

1. The questions were asked of all respondents who attend religious services a few times a year or less, including those who self-identify as Christians, those who identify with other religions, and religious "nones" (i.e., those who identify, religiously, as atheist, agnostic or "nothing in particular"). The questions employed neutral phrasing—they asked about why respondents attend "religious services" a few times a year or less, not why respondents attend "church" a few times a year or less—so as to be applicable to all such groups, not just Christians. However, since most US adults identify as Christians, this report sometimes uses phrases like "church attenders" as shorthand for those who attend religious services regularly. Full question wording is available in the topline.

2. Respondents were able to cite more than one reason as "very important" for why they attend religious services. Overall, 88% of respondents who attend religious services at least once or twice a month indicated that more than one reason is "very important."

3. The survey did not include a question that asked those who rarely or never attend religious services about the most important reason they refrain from doing so.

4. This includes both those who named only becoming "closer to God" as a "very important" reason for attending religious services, as well as those who named more than one reason as "very important" and then indicated, in the follow-up question, that becoming closer to God is the most important reason they attend religious services. Other categories are calculated the same way.

5. These categories are not mutually exclusive; for example, some respondents who say "I practice my faith in other ways" is a very important reason they do not attend religious services also say "I don't feel welcome" is a very important reason.

For Many Americans, Self-Care Just Isn't Enough

Kristi Pahr

Kristi Pahr is a freelance writer who has published work in various publications, including the New York Times, Real Simple, *and* Men's Health.

A few months ago, I decided to make some changes in my life to address my problems with anxiety.

I told my husband I was going to do one thing every day just for myself. I called it radical self-care, and I felt very good about it. I have two little kids and don't get much time to myself, so the idea of doing one thing just for me, every single day, certainly felt radical.

I jumped in with both feet, insisting on taking a walk or spending time doing yoga or even just sitting alone on the porch to read a book every day. Nothing extreme, nothing Instagrammable. Just 20 minutes of calm every day . . .

And at the end of the first week, I found myself sitting in the bathroom bawling and trembling and hyperventilating—having a full-on anxiety attack—because it was time for my "radical self-care."

Needless to say, those were not the results I was expecting. It was just supposed to be a walk, but it sent me spiraling and I couldn't do it.

For lots of folks with anxiety disorders, this kind of "self-care" just doesn't work.

Self-Care Is Having a Moment

These days, self-care is touted as a balm for everything that ails you: from stress and insomnia, all the way to chronic physical illnesses,

"For Many People with Anxiety, Self-Care Just Doesn't Work," by Kristi Pahr, Healthline Media, June 12, 2018. Reprinted by permission.

or mental illnesses like OCD and depression. Somewhere, someone is saying that self-care is exactly what you need to feel better.

And in many cases, it is.

Taking a break and doing something nice for yourself is good for you. Self-care *can* be a balm. But it isn't always.

Sometimes, doing something for yourself just makes it worse, especially if you live with an anxiety disorder.

Roughly 20 percent of US adults live with some sort of anxiety disorder, making it the most prevalent mental illness in the United States. So many people have anxiety, and so many people are finally talking about anxiety, that—for me at least—it feels like the stigma is starting to lift a little.

And with that openness and acceptance comes the prescriptive advice we often see filling up our newsfeeds—from the ever-present wellness articles to wholesome memes, much of which involve some sort of affirmation as self-care.

For many people with anxiety disorders, a trip to the spa, a nap, or an hour of people watching in the park might be something they really want to do—or feel like they *should* do. They try because they think they're supposed to, or that it will help them get their thoughts under control and stop worrying about everything.

But it doesn't help them feel better. It doesn't stop the swirl of worry and anxiety and stress. It doesn't help them focus or calm down.

For lots of folks with anxiety disorders, this kind of "self-care" just doesn't work.

According to California therapist, Melinda Haynes, "Taking time to administer a healthy dose of self-care can trigger feelings of guilt (I *should be* working/cleaning/spending more time with my kids), or stir up unresolved feelings related to self-worth (I don't deserve this or I'm not good enough for this)."

And this pretty much ruins the idea of self-care being helpful—it moves it over into the trigger category.

Haynes explains that people who live with anxiety "typically cannot experience the simplicity or peace of 'just self.' There are too many to-dos and what-ifs flooding the mind and body at any given moment. Taking a timeout from the busy pace of life only highlights this irregularity . . . hence, the guilt or low self-worth."

#Selfcare #Obsession

In our increasingly connected lives, social media platforms like Facebook and Instagram have become indispensable. We use them for work, for keeping in touch with friends and family, for shopping, for learning new things. But we also use them to show the world what we're up to. We document and hashtag everything, even our self-care.

Especially our self-care.

"Self-care is fetishised and has become instagrammable," Dr. Perpetua Neo explains. "People think there are checkboxes to tick, standards to upkeep, and yet they don't understand why they do what they do."

"If you find yourself obsessing over the 'correct way' to self-care, and feel like crap consistently after it, then it's a big sign to stop," she adds.

We can even search our social media to see what other people are doing to care for themselves — the hashtags are plentiful.

#Selflove #Selfcare #Wellness #Wellbing

Dr. Kelsey Latimer, from the Center for Discovery in Florida, points out that "self-care would most likely not be associated with posting to social media unless it was a spontaneous post, as self-care is focused on being in the moment and tuning out the social pressures."

And the social pressures around wellness are numerous.

The wellness industry has created space for improved mental health, yes, but it's also morphed into just another way to be perfect—"like it's easy to have the perfect diet, perfect body, and yes—even the perfect self-care routine."

Latimer explains: "This in itself takes us out of the self-care process and into the pressure zone."

If you feel strongly about developing a self-care practice, but don't know how to make it work for you, discuss it with a mental health professional and work together to come up with a plan that helps instead of harms.

If it's watching TV, watch TV. If it's a bath, take a bath. If it's sipping a unicorn latte, doing an hour of hot yoga, then sitting for a reiki session, do it. Your self-care is your business.

My experiment in radical self-care evolved over time. I stopped trying to *do* self-care,I stopped pushing it. I stopped doing what other people said *should* make me feel better and started doing what I *know* makes me feel better.

Your self-care doesn't have to look like anyone else's. It doesn't need to have a hashtag. It just needs to be whatever makes you feel good.

Take care of yourself, even if that means skipping all the bells and whistles and not stressing yourself out. Because *that* is self-care too.

Living Alone Doesn't Mean Someone Is Socially Isolated

Claude S. Fischer

Claude Fischer is a professor of sociology at the University of California, Berkeley. He is also the author of Made in America: A Social History of American Culture and Character.

I t is common to read that the percentage of Americans who live by themselves has increased substantially over the last few decades. It is often the first or second observation in an essay arguing—assuming—that Americans have become more isolated and lonely.

But there are substantial misunderstandings about who lives alone, why they live alone, and what kind of social life those living alone lead. Some types of people who live alone are actually more social than those who share a household.

The Trend

A common mistake writers make is to take the easily available statistics on how many American *homes* have a single resident—in 1960 13% and in 2008 *28%* of homes, over 1 in 4, had only one resident—and to remark on how much living alone has expanded. But that is not the statistic we want. We're not interested in what's happened to *homes*; we're interested in what's happened to *people*. The percentage of American adults who lived alone in 2008 was 15%, which is a lot less.

Yet, that, too, increased. Around 1900, a few percent of Americans lived by themselves; in 1960, 6% did; and now about 15% do.

"Alone or Lonely?" by Claude Fischer, *Made in America*, August 11, 2010. Reprinted by permission.

The Reason

Who lives alone? And why? In 2009, one-fourth of those who lived alone were women 65 and older. It is the elderly who are especially likely to live alone. Sorting by age and sex, 25% of men 75 years old and older lived alone in 2009 and 49%, *about half*, of women 75 and older—lived alone. (Remember: This is compared to 15% of all adults.) Living alone is largely what Americans do who live long enough to outlive their spouses. And this explains most of the growth in single-person households over the last several decades.

(By the way, do these widows and widowers live alone voluntarily or because their children won't have them? The evidence strongly shows that the elderly prefer to live alone when they physically and financially can. The elderly are, for example, *more* likely than young people to tell pollsters that old people living with their adult children is not a good idea.)

Another, smaller component in the expansion of solo-living is the delay of marriage since about 1960. More Americans are waiting longer to marry. And increasingly, many of the single twenty- and young thirty-somethings who once would have stayed with their parents until they faced the preacher now either live alone if they can afford to or with roommates if they cannot until the wedding bells toll.

A third, yet smaller, component of the solo-livers are the divorced—especially divorced men. (Divorced women typically live with children.) Here, we start to get larger proportions of people in single households who would prefer not to live alone. But the divorced, especially the men, do not stay divorced long, a couple of years or so on average, although longer for women.

Most scholars who have studied this topic suggest a much greater proportion of Americans start living alone, especially after the 1960s, because it became much more affordable to do so—incomes rose, income security increased, and housing options grew—at least until the last couple of decades. In an earlier era, for example, divorced women and their children would often move back to their parents' home; that has become rarer. (Whether the current economic catastrophe is reversing the trend and sending people back to sharing homes we will know in a few years.)

Some scholars argue that Americans' wish to be alone, to cut ties, also grew over the century. Perhaps, but that is not where most of the research points.

No More Boarders

Another place to see the move to residential independence is the virtual end of rooming and boarding. Back around 1900, about 3 percent of Americans (5 percent of men)—many of them immigrant workers and the poor elderly who lacked adult children to live with—roomed or boarded in someone's home. And about one of 10 households took in boarders, commonly, households run by needy widows.

Today, only about one-half of one percent of Americans are roomers or boarders (despite a small surge in rooming among Hispanics) and those few are increasingly students rather than workers or the elderly.

It appears that for both would-be boarders and would-be boarding-householders (notably, widows), it has become easier to live alone.

Alone or Lonely?

In the common telling, writers equate living alone with being alone and lonely. Equating the two is essentially wrong.

Some people who live alone feel lonely because they lack a romantic partner; specifically that is the source of their loneliness. As Roy Orbison sang, "Now only the lonely/ Know the heartaches I've been through/ Only the lonely/ Know I cry and cry for you." The issue is not household arrangements; the issue is love. We should not confuse the two.

And some people who live alone (especially old men) are truly isolated, lacking much contact with others.

But, on the whole and other things being equal, people who live alone have, on average, about as many friends and as active a social life—if not more—than people like themselves who do not live alone. (Quick side point: The singles do *not* have more sex. Research shows that married people have more sex; there is a benefit to convenience.) If you bracket some of the travails that are correlated with living alone—such as getting divorced; such as getting very old, which typically means getting frailer and having your friends die off—then solo living by itself does not seem to contribute much either to social isolation or feeling lonely.

One probable reason it does not is that people who live alone have fewer at-home commitments—spouses, children, roommates—that inhibit social life. For young singles in particular, the period they live alone is also a period of exploration and adventure. Getting married and having kids, research shows, lead people, notably women, to lose touch with some of their friends. At the same time, research on widows often notes that many of them, although certainly grieving, attain more of a social life when they are no longer caring for an ill or disabled spouse.

Feeling lonely is a serious issue; it is associated with depression. But living alone and feeling lonely are two different things. Also, living alone has increased—but loneliness, according to the data, has not—a topic for a later post.

Self-Care Can Keep Psychological Distress at Bay

Nicole Chanway

Nicole Chanway has blogged about mental health, including self-care, as a student at the University of British Columbia in Canada. She has served as a liaison worker for the Urban Indigenous Health and Healing Cooperative in Vancouver, British Columbia. The organization provides a decolonized approach to health care.

The term "self-care" is one you've probably heard a lot lately. It's often tossed around campus as something to keep in mind, something to make sure you don't forget, and yet in these brief mentions, it's usually treated as something of an afterthought. It may be something your professor indirectly mentions by telling your class to be sure to get a good sleep and be well-rested for the midterm the next day. Getting enough sleep is, of course, crucial, but there are further elements to self-care than just a healthy sleep cycle, and these elements are often left by the wayside.

The thing is, looking after your mental well-being should be a priority, and self-care is a great way to address that need. It quickly becomes pretty impossible to balance writing papers, studying for midterms, seeing friends, and Skyping home on a regular basis when you aren't taking proper care of yourself. What's more, a lack of attention to your mental well-being can speedily and stealthily spill over until it affects your physical health. Take it from a seasoned and only slightly world-weary fourth year English honours student: practice self-care. Seriously. Do it.

"So tell me, Nicole," you might be thinking, "how exactly do I practice self-care, if it's so important?"

"Mental Stealth: Self-Care 101," Nicole Chanway, The University of British Columbia, February 14, 2018. https://learningcommons.ubc.ca/mental-stealth-self-care-101/. Licensed under CC BY-ND 4.0 International.

Herein lies the problem: self-care is different for everyone. Even though this misleading little number is entitled Self-Care 101, there's no textbook for this class, and there are no right answers. Whatever feels good, healthy, and restorative to you is your unique recipe for good self-care.

Pretty unhelpful, right? Never fear. Instead of prescribing self-care methods and writing about what I feel is the best way to practice self-care, I'm going to share some important aspects of my own self-care routine. Self-care is anything but a one-size-fits-all model, but at the very least, maybe some of my methods can inspire you to discover your own.

- Exercise: I know this is old news, but exercise works wonders. I'm a recent convert to this method of self-care. I used to brush off the sentiment that even going for a quick walk and getting some fresh air improves one's mental state, but I now see how true this is for me. I love strolling through my neighbourhood (when it isn't too rainy), and I visit the aquatic centre gym (which is free with your UBC card) three times a week. I always feel energized and ready to handle whatever life throws at me after I've had a chance to be active.
- Reading: As an English student, a lot of my homework is completing readings (and then writing about the readings I did). I try to keep this kind of reading separate from the reading I do for fun. For me, reading is an excellent way to escape for a few hours, and when I come back to the real world, I feel refreshed.
- Netflix: Yes, I consider Netflix and its brethren to be self-care. Sometimes what my brain really needs at the end of a long day is for me to shut my textbooks and put on a movie. There are times when nothing makes me feel more mentally and emotionally healthy than getting into my comfiest sweater and curling up in bed with an episode of *Orange Is the New Black.*
- Conversation: Sometimes what I need for my self-care is an in-depth talk with a close friend about something I'm

experiencing, or sometimes even just a friendly and casual interaction with a cashier will put a smile on my face. It's easy for me to get wrapped up in the world of studying and papers and forget every so often how crucial human interaction is to my health and happiness.

- Good food: It's tough to find time to cook, but I've learned pretty recently that it's worth prioritizing sometimes. Though time and money are always factors in what I eat, I invariably feel better, physically and mentally, when I've gone the extra mile and cooked something healthy and tasty. I also find the physical process of putting together a meal to be highly therapeutic, especially when I'm listening to my favourite songs as I'm chopping vegetables.

I encourage you to explore the things that make you feel happy, safe, and healthy. Self-care is a highly individual action, and it's possible that these five types of self-care I've listed may not appeal to you at all. That's totally fine—we all look after ourselves in different ways. Just make sure that you are, after all, finding time to look after yourself!

Some Religious People Still Don't Understand Mental Illness

Amanda Holpuch

Amanda Holpuch is a national correspondent for the Guardian. *She has written about US politics as well as issues affecting Canada and Mexico. She lives in New York City.*

Carlos Whittaker, a prominent evangelical writer and musician, was singing worship songs on stage in 2005 when he suddenly felt like he was having a heart attack and that he would soon die. An audience of 2,000 people watched, and the band played on, as Whittaker left the stage, not knowing that he was having a panic attack.

Though some people still tell Whittaker that his anxiety could be improved if he would just make his faith stronger and pray more, evangelical leaders and grassroots activists are orchestrating a shift in the way the community approaches mental health issues.

"This has nothing to with whether I believe in Jesus," Whittaker told the *Guardian*. "This does not have anything to do with whether or not I am reading my Bible or how hard I am praying. I can pray 24 hours a day, seven days a week, and I'm still going to have to take that little white pill every single day."

That little white pill is 20mg of Paxil, and Whittaker has taken it every day for the past nine years to treat anxiety. Of all the controversial topics he speaks about in public, he said mental health is the one that elicits the most responses from his fellow evangelicals—and it's not always positive.

Whittaker started blogging about his mental health struggles in 2007, only to be told by his pastor that he should stop talking about them. In the last two or three years, though, he says he's noticed

"Christians and Mental Health: 'This Has Nothing to Do with Whether I Believe in Jesus,'" by Amanda Holpuch, Guardian News & Media Limited, November 13, 2014. Reprinted by permission.

the evangelical community becoming more open to mental health discussions. "I am watching more and more people come out of the clinical depression closet and talk about it," Whittaker said.

Part of what mental health campaigners must overcome is the evangelical idea that demons, bad spirits or sin are causing the mental illness and that it can be prayed away. Lifeway Research, an evangelical research firm based in Nashville, released a study last year that said nearly half of evangelical Christians believe that people with serious mental disorders can overcome their illness with "Bible study and prayer alone."

The battle to approach mental healthcare from a more scientific perspective has long been waged by individuals within the community, but now an effort to change this perception is coming from church leaders.

Megachurch pastor Rick Warren took up the cause after his son Matthew killed himself in April 2013. In March, Warren held a day-long conference on mental health at the Lake Forest, California, campus of his Saddleback Church, which has an average attendance of more than 22,000 people. Saddleback is partnering with the American Foundation for Suicide Prevention on 22 November to host an event for people who have lost someone to suicide and who would like to learn more about how to prevent it.

Frank Page, the former president of the Southern Baptist Convention, in 2013 published a book about his daughter's suicide in an effort to raise awareness about how churches could better work with people who have mental health issues.

To some, this would seem to be a turn from the conservative values often associated with evangelicals. "The picture of evangelicals as being judgmental, harsh and living in a bubble community—while that might be true of some, the landscape has changed dramatically towards inclusion, dialogue and care," said Marcia Pally, a New York University professor and author of *The New Evangelicals*.

She said the evangelical movement was once progressive and at times "quite radical" until it took a turn to the right in the late 1960s. But the political landscape of evangelicalism has shifted since George W. Bush's second term as president, with more members engaging in a broad spectrum of activism about things which would be considered progressive.

Pally said that because leaders like Warren have more of the spotlight, it gives them more influence on the movement. But for social change to occur, that has to be balanced with local and grassroots efforts, particularly among evangelicals. "Nobody will take on a position or cause just because someone said they should; people have their own beliefs, consciences and community sensibilities," she said.

These evangelical grassroots efforts are gaining traction as community churches build mental health ministries. The Ankeny First United Methodist Church, just outside Des Moines, Iowa, started a mental health ministry three years ago after congregants told church leaders that they were not doing enough to support mental health concerns.

"Nearly everybody has a family member that is having mental health issues and nobody wants to talk about it," said Jaque Coulson, the church's director of care and connection. "It can be freeing, in a sense, to have a safe place to talk about it."

The National Alliance on Mental Illness gave Iowa, and 20 other states, its second-to-worst rating for mental health care. Ankeny Methodist's mental health ministry also works with secular community groups to improve services across the region. Coulson said the group's top request for 2015 is to have people come in and educate them on how to be involved in the legislative process.

Mental health professionals are also working to better understand how religion can be a part of their care. Researchers conducted a review of this relationship, concluding that the mental health professionals and religious groups are "moving from a period of 'antagonism' to 'mutual understanding.'"

The Department of Veterans Affairs is researching this relationship to see how it could improve veteran mental healthcare, especially as the concept of "moral injury" becomes more accepted in the psychology world.

Jeffrey Pyne, a psychiatrist at the VA and the University of Arkansas who worked on the review, said that in a pilot study, veterans explained how they feel like they have nowhere to turn. "Some of them will say: 'I know what I need, I need forgiveness, but I don't think my mental health provider is going to provide that for me. And I don't even feel worthy to go to a chaplain to ask for forgiveness,' so they are stuck," said Pyne.

He said that addressing the issues of guilt and shame-based fear does not have to be constrained to evangelical approaches and that researchers are examining how other religions deal with these issues.

Dr. Keith Meador works in the intersection of theology and mental health at Vanderbilt University and the department of Veterans Affairs. One reason he thinks religion should be considered more frequently by mental health advocates is because it can be a part of the social element of a person's wellbeing. "I can't explain how many times have I yearned, though the worst of the patient's depression might be over, what I really wanted to do is write a prescription for a community, a place to belong," said Meador.

The American Psychiatric Association in July participated in a meeting of more than 40 prominent researchers and representatives of multiple religions to discuss how mental health professionals and religious groups could work together.

Dr. Paul Summergrad, president of the American Psychiatric Association and psychiatrist-in-chief at Tufts medical center, said it is important for the mental health side to be open to working with clergy because when people in the US are experiencing mental illness, many first turn to their religious community for help.

"We are in general moving to be being more open to talk about these conditions," Summergrad said. "And the more they become visible, and the more there is sunlight on them, the less there will be stigma and people will recognize that these are things lots of people suffer with and that lots of people can get better."

Chapter 2

Are People with Mental Illnesses Stigmatized in the United States?

More Needs to Be Learned About Stigma and Mental Illness

Patrick W. Corrigan and Amy C. Watson

Patrick W. Corrigan is distinguished professor of psychology at the Illinois Institute of Technology and principal investigator of the National Consortium for Stigma and Empowerment, a collective of mental health advocates. Amy C. Watson is a professor in the Jane Addams College of Social Work at the University of Illinois at Chicago. Before her move to academia, she served as a probation officer in DuPage County, Illinois, for five years. In this capacity, she mostly worked with people with mental illness.

M any people with serious mental illness are challenged doubly. On one hand, they struggle with the symptoms and disabilities that result from the disease. On the other, they are challenged by the stereotypes and prejudice that result from misconceptions about mental illness. As a result of both, people with mental illness are robbed of the opportunities that define a quality life: good jobs, safe housing, satisfactory health care, and affiliation with a diverse group of people. Although research has gone far to understand the impact of the disease, it has only recently begun to explain stigma in mental illness. Much work yet needs to be done to fully understand the breadth and scope of prejudice against people with mental illness. Fortunately, social psychologists and sociologists have been studying phenomena related to stigma in other minority groups for several decades. In this paper, we integrate research specific to mental illness stigma with the more general body of research on stereotypes and prejudice to provide a brief overview of issues in the area.

"Understanding the Impact of Stigma on People with Mental Illness," by Patrick W. Corrigan and Amy C. Watson, *World Psychiatry* 2002 Feb; 1(1): 16–20. Reprinted by permission."

The impact of stigma is twofold. Public stigma is the reaction that the general population has to people with mental illness. Self-stigma is the prejudice which people with mental illness turn against themselves. Both public and self-stigma may be understood in terms of three components: stereotypes, prejudice, and discrimination. Social psychologists view stereotypes as especially efficient, social knowledge structures that are learned by most members of a social group. Stereotypes are considered "social" because they represent collectively agreed upon notions of groups of persons. They are "efficient" because people can quickly generate impressions and expectations of individuals who belong to a stereotyped group.

Public Stigma

Stigmas about mental illness seem to be widely endorsed by the general public in the Western world. Studies suggest that the majority of citizens in the United States and many Western European nations have stigmatizing attitudes about mental illness. Furthermore, stigmatizing views about mental illness are not limited to uninformed members of the general public; even well-trained professionals from most mental health disciplines subscribe to stereotypes about mental illness.

Stigma seems to be less evident in Asian and African countries, though it is unclear whether this finding represents a cultural sphere that does not promote stigma or a dearth of research in these societies. The available research indicates that, while attitudes toward mental illness vary among non-Western cultures, the stigma of mental illness may be less severe than in Western cultures. Horacio Fabrega suggests that the lack of differentiation between psychiatric and non-psychiatric illness in the three great non-Western medical traditions is an important factor. While the potential for stigmatization of psychiatric illness certainly exists in non-Western cultures, it seems to primarily attach to the more chronic forms of illness that fail to respond to traditional treatments. Notably, stigma seems almost nonexistent in Islamic societies. Cross-cultural examinations of the concepts, experiences, and responses to mental illness are clearly needed.

Several themes describe misconceptions about mental illness and corresponding stigmatizing attitudes. Media analyses of film and print have identified three: people with mental illness are homicidal maniacs who need to be feared; they have childlike perceptions of the world that should be marveled; or they are responsible for their illness because they have weak character. Results of two independent factor analyses of the survey responses of more than 2000 English and American citizens parallel these findings:

- fear and exclusion: persons with severe mental illness should be feared and, therefore, be kept out of most communities;
- authoritarianism: persons with severe mental illness are irresponsible, so life decisions should be made by others;
- benevolence: persons with severe mental illness are childlike and need to be cared for.

Although stigmatizing attitudes are not limited to mental illness, the public seems to disapprove persons with psychiatric disabilities significantly more than persons with related conditions such as physical illness. Severe mental illness has been likened to drug addiction, prostitution, and criminality. Unlike physical disabilities, persons with mental illness are perceived by the public to be in control of their disabilities and responsible for causing them. Furthermore, research respondents are less likely to pity persons with mental illness, instead reacting to psychiatric disability with anger and believing that help is not deserved.

The behavioral impact (or discrimination) that results from public stigma may take four forms: withholding help, avoidance, coercive treatment, and segregated institutions. Previous studies have shown that the public will withhold help to some minority groups because of corresponding stigma. A more extreme form of this behavior is social avoidance, where the public strives to not interact with people with mental illness altogether. The

1996 General Social Survey (GSS), in which the Mac Arthur Mental Health Module was administered to a probability sample of 1444 adults in the United States, found that more than a half of respondents are unwilling to: spend an evening socializing, work next to, or have a family member marry a person with mental illness. Social avoidance is not just self-report; it is also a reality. Research has shown that stigma has a deleterious impact on obtaining good jobs and leasing safe housing.

Discrimination can also appear in public opinion about how to treat people with mental illness. For example, though recent studies have been unable to demonstrate the effectiveness of mandatory treatment, more than 40% of the 1996 GSS sample agreed that people with schizophrenia should be forced into treatment. Additionally, the public endorses segregation in institutions as the best service for people with serious psychiatric disorders.

Strategies for Changing Public Stigma

Change strategies for public stigma have been grouped into three approaches: protest, education, and contact. Groups protest inaccurate and hostile representations of mental illness as a way to challenge the stigmas they represent. These efforts send two messages. To the media: STOP reporting inaccurate representations of mental illness. To the public: STOP believing negative views about mental illness. Otto F. Wahl believes citizens are encountering far fewer sanctioned examples of stigma and stereotypes because of protest efforts. Anecdotal evidence suggests that protest campaigns have been effective in getting stigmatizing images of mental illness withdrawn. There is, however, little empirical research on the psychological impact of protest campaigns on stigma and discrimination, suggesting an important direction for future research.

Protest is a reactive strategy; it attempts to diminish negative attitudes about mental illness, but fails to promote more positive attitudes that are supported by facts. Education provides information so that the public can make more informed decisions about mental illness. This approach to changing stigma has been most thoroughly examined by investigators. Research, for example, has suggested that persons who evince a better understanding of mental illness are less likely to endorse stigma and discrimination. Hence, the strategic provision of information about mental illness seems to lessen negative stereotypes. Several studies have shown that participation in education programs on mental illness led to improved attitudes about persons with these problems. Education programs are effective for a wide variety of participants, including college undergraduates, graduate students, adolescents, community residents, and persons with mental illness.

Stigma is further diminished when members of the general public meet persons with mental illness who are able to hold down jobs or live as good neighbors in the community. Research has shown an inverse relationship between having contact with a person with mental illness and endorsing psychiatric stigma. Hence, opportunities for the public to meet persons with severe mental illness may discount stigma. Interpersonal contact is further enhanced when the general public is able to regularly interact with people with mental illness as peers.

Self-Stigma

One might think that people with psychiatric disability, living in a society that widely endorses stigmatizing ideas, will internalize these ideas and believe that they are less valued because of their psychiatric disorder. Self-esteem suffers, as does confidence in one's future. Given this research, models of self-stigma need to account for the deleterious effects of prejudice on an individual's conception of him or herself. However, research also suggests that, instead of being diminished by the stigma, many persons become righteously angry because of the prejudice that they have experienced. This kind of reaction empowers people to change their roles in the mental health system, becoming more active participants in their treatment plan and often pushing for improvements in the quality of services.

Low self-esteem versus righteous anger describes a fundamental paradox in self-stigma. Models that explain the experience of self-stigma need to account for some persons whose sense of self is harmed by social stigma versus others who are energized by, and forcefully react to, the injustice. And there is yet a third group that needs to be considered in describing the impact of stigma on the self. The sense of self for many persons with mental illness is neither hurt, nor energized, by social stigma, instead showing a seeming indifference to it altogether.

We propose a situational model that explains this paradox, arguing that an individual with mental illness may experience diminished self-esteem/self-efficacy, righteous anger, or relative indifference depending on the parameters of the situation. Important factors that affect a situational response to stigma include collective representations that are primed in that situation, the person's perception of the legitimacy of stigma in the situation, and the person's identification with the larger group of individuals with mental illness. This model has eventual implications for ways in which persons with mental illness might cope with self-stigma as well as identification of policies that promote environments in which stigma festers.

Misconceptions About Therapy Linger in Some Communities

Monnica T. Williams

Dr. Monnica T. Williams is a clinical psychologist and associate professor in the department of psychological sciences at the University of Connecticut. She also serves as director of the university's Laboratory for Culture and Mental Health Disparities and as clinical director of the Behavioral Wellness Clinic in Tolland, Connecticut.

African Americans share the same mental health issues as the rest of the population, with arguably even greater stressors due to racism, prejudice, and economic disparities. Meanwhile, many wonder why African Americans shy away from psychotherapy as a potential solution to challenges such as depression, anxiety, post-traumatic stress disorder, marriage problems, and parenting issues. As a Black psychologist, it is troublesome that so many African Americans are reluctant to make use of psychology's solutions to emotional hurdles. Here are some of the issues I've encountered in my research and clinical practice, with practical ideas for addressing this disparity.

Stigma and Judgment

In places like Los Angeles and New York, everyone and their pet has a therapist, yet even among the wealthy and elite, many African Americans continue to hold stigmatizing beliefs about mental illness. For example, a qualitative study by Alvidrez et al., (2008) found that among Blacks who were already mental health consumers, over a third felt that mild depression or anxiety would be considered "crazy" in their social circles. Talking about problems with an outsider (i.e., therapist) may be viewed as airing one's "dirty laundry," and even more telling is the fact that over a quarter of

"Why African Americans Avoid Psychotherapy," by Monnica T Williams Ph.D., *Psychology Today*, Sussex Publishers, LLC, November 2, 2011. Reprinted by permission.

those consumers felt that discussions about mental illness would not be appropriate even among family.

In a study I recently completed, one African American gentleman noted, "I was just embarrassed. Getting this type of help has, and continues to be, like a sore thumb in the African American community. Unfortunately, I don't have insurance, so my fear was that if I sought help, it would not be good because I couldn't afford it."

Likewise, African Americans may be resistant to seek treatment because they fear it may reflect badly on their families—an outward admission of the family's failure to handle problems internally. Something I found in my own studies, is that even among African Americans who suffered greatly from mental disorders, many held negative attitudes about people who obtain mental health care. No matter how impaired they were, they didn't want to be one of "those people."

Many African Americans with mental disorders are unaware that they have a diagnosable illness at all, and are even less aware that effective psychological treatments exist for their specific problem. Because of the taboo surrounding open discussion about mental illness, African Americans often have little knowledge of mental health problems and their treatments.

Concerns About Therapist or Treatment Process

Many African Americans also have concerns about treatment effectiveness, which may be due to both lack of education and cultural misgivings. Apprehension about clashing with the values or worldview of the clinician can cause ambivalence about seeking help, and this may be especially true for the many who believe that mental health treatment was designed by White people for White people. African Americans view the typical psychologist as an older, White male, who would be insensitive to the social and economic realities of their lives. In actuality, however, even though African Americans are underrepresented as psychologists, they are well-represented among mental health providers in general, and can be found among the ranks of master's level clinicians, such as professional counselors and clinical social workers. These types of therapists can be very useful for many sorts of difficulties, including family problems and many mental health needs.

Anxiety about therapy may also be related to a lack of knowledge about what to expect from the treatment itself. Indeed, many African Americans with mental disorders express fears about being involuntarily hospitalized, and are unwilling to share their symptoms for fear of being "locked up" or "put away."

Yet even those who are willing to brave treatment may not place therapy among their priorities. Work, family responsibilities, commitments, and transportation issues all can overshadow the need for therapy, which may be viewed as a luxury endeavor when there are kids to drive to little league and dinner to make at home. This troublesome reality suggests that despite struggling for years with a mental disorder, many are reluctant to take time for themselves to get better.

Cost of Treatment and Lack of Insurance Coverage

The financial burden of mental health treatment is a barrier that affects everyone, but disproportionally affects African Americans due to lower incomes and reduced employment opportunities. In my own research, I found that those most concerned about cost are more likely to be uninsured; their incomes are not low enough to qualify for publicly provided services but not high enough to afford a private insurance plan.

Increasing Treatment Participation

All of the issues described thus far can create a difficult uphill battle when trying to increase treatment participation within the African American community. But there are many practical approaches that can reduce this mental health disparity.

Making Treatment More Affordable

The cost of treatment may be prohibitive for many, especially among those without insurance coverage. Many low-income individuals can find help in the community health system, but such systems may suffer from a lack of clinicians able to treat complex and less common conditions. It can be especially difficult to find care for those who lack any sort of insurance, have an unstable living situation, or who must contend with the inability to make appointments due to overcrowding.

Individual practices and treatment centers can help by publicizing effective low cost treatment options (*i.e.* practicum students, sliding scale slots, etc.). Another cost-effective option is stepped-care. For example, one model proposed by Tolin, Diefenback, Maltby, and Hannan, (2005) for the treatment of OCD involves bibliotherapy (self-help books), followed by clinician-guided self-treatment as needed, as well as traditional exposure and ritual prevention for non-responders. In this way, the most expensive treatment is provided to those who need it most, while others may benefit from a lesser approach. Nonetheless, it is important to be aware that the cost of treatment is a larger problem that involves many aspects of our society, including the politics of health care and social inequalities.

Increasing Awareness of Mental Disorders
and Treatment Options

Education about mental disorders and the treatment process is a critical step to reducing barriers to treatment among the African American community. Suggestions for overcoming this barrier include public education campaigns (e.g., mass media), educational presentations at community venues (e.g., Black churches), and open information sessions at local mental health clinics. In fact, many Black churches are taking the treatment to where the people are, and hiring licensed therapists to work with their flock.

For those who do start conventional treatment, the first clinical encounter presents an important opportunity to address skepticism about the usefulness of treatment. It's the clinician's responsibility to demystify the process and explain the benefits of staying the course. Without this knowledge the participant may only assume what he or she may encounter and base their decision to follow through on incorrect assumptions. If the expected outcomes, number of sessions, and potential goals are clearly outlined in advance, there is little chance of feeling misled or not in control. The client-patient bond may be strengthened with this extra attempt at transparency.

Making Mental Health a Priority

Treatment has the potential to conflict with many daily activities or commitments for busy people. In the current economy, many take second and third jobs to make ends meet. Whether the individual feels treatment is a necessary priority despite prior engagements, transportation, or scheduling issues is an important positive step. Moreover, incorporating the family is another crucial measure in overcoming barriers to treatment. By gaining familial support the client may gain peace of mind as well as lose the fear of being outcast or stigmatized. In addition, with the family's acceptance, making time for treatment becomes easier and priorities may be put into perspective. Utilizing the family to emphasize the importance of good mental health creates more allies to emphasize the relationship between improved functioning and greater success at home and work.

Reducing Fears About Therapy and Stigma

Making psychotherapy less intimidating may be one of the most important ways of improving help-seeking. Careful use of language can help to reduce some discomfort surrounding mental health care. For example, African Americans are more comfortable with the term "counseling" over "psychotherapy," and this should be considered in advertising and conversational exchanges. Another practical way to reduce fears is to offer free assessments and phone consultations, which will help familiarize potential patients with the clinic, clinician, and treatment. Clinicians might use initial contacts to address fears of being involuntarily hospitalized by explaining the difference between typical mental health challenges and "being crazy," including the role of insight and self-efficacy.

However, it is important to note that reservations against treatment may be rooted in actual experiences of racism and encounters with medical professionals lacking cultural awareness. Treatment is a partnership that can only be successful with mutual respect, and for this to occur it remains the duty of the therapist to become culturally competent and sensitive to disparities, and in turn, communicate support and understanding to the patient. African Americans look for subtle cues to determine if a therapist holds racist attitudes, as many are afraid of being mistreated due to their race or ethnicity. These concerns are not unfounded, as a lower social status makes African Americans more vulnerable to abuse, particularly in a medical setting, where the clinician is considered the authority figure. A recent study by Snowden et al. found that after controlling for severity of mental illness and other variables, African Americans are more than twice as likely to experience a psychiatric hospitalization than Whites, an indication of continued bias among clinicians when faced with Black patients in need of mental health services.

To completely eliminate mental health disparities, clinicians must be willing to undertake an honest self-examination of their own conscious and unconscious attitudes about race, including preconceived notions about who would be a good client. By increasing the cultural competence and social awareness of all clinicians, the mental health system can begin to shed its bias against ethnic minorities. This would result in greater understanding and empathy for the patient's experience, improved treatment outcomes, and more African Americans willing to take a chance with mental health care.

How Cultural Attitudes Contribute to Stigmatization of Mental Illness

Judy Baker

Judy Baker is a dean at Foothill College in Los Altos Hills, California. She earned her doctorate in health education from the University of Texas and her master's degree in social work from Virginia Commonwealth University. She has taught a variety of community health courses at both the graduate and undergraduate level.

Culture can be defined in terms of the shared knowledge, beliefs, and values that characterize a social group. Humans have a strong drive to maintain the sense of identity that comes from membership in an identifiable group. In primeval and nomadic times, a person's survival likely benefited from establishing strong bonds with an in-group of trusted relatives or clan-mates with whom one co-operated and shared, versus an out-group against which there was competition for scarce resources. Within the intermixing of modern society, many of us seek to retain a sense of cultural identity and may often refer to our cultural roots, or use double-barreled descriptions such as Asian-American. It is important that we are all aware of our own cultural influences and how these may affect our perceptions of others, especially in the doctor-patient encounter. In many subtle ways, the cultural identities of both doctor and patient affect their interaction, and in a diverse country this can form an exciting challenge.

Culture and Individual

We all perceive others through the filter or perspective of our own cultural upbringing, often without being aware of it: communication can go wrong without our understanding why. The clinician must

"Culture, Beliefs, Attitudes, and Stigmatized Illness," by Judy Baker, PhD, Lumen Learning, 2007. https://courses.lumenlearning.com/diseaseprevention/chapter/culture-beliefs-attitudes-and-stigmatized-illnesses/. Licensed under CC BY-SA 4.0 International.

become culturally aware and sensitive, then culturally competent so that she or he can practice in a manner that is culturally safe.

Cultural Awareness

Cultural competency in medical practice requires that the clinician respects and appreciates diversity in society. Culturally competent clinicians acknowledge differences but do not feel threatened by them. "Culturally competent communication leaves our patients feeling that their concerns were understood, a trusting relationship was formed and, above all, that they were treated with respect." While a clinician will often be unfamiliar with the culture of a particular patient, the direct approach is often the best: ask the patient what you need to understand about her culture and background in order to be able to help her. A direct approach helps establish mutual respect and tailor the best and most appropriate care for each patient.

Awareness of one's own culture is an important step towards awareness of, and sensitivity to, the culture and ethnicity of other people. Clinicians who are not aware of their own cultural biases may unconsciously impose their cultural values on other people. "As physicians, we must make multiple communication adjustments each day when interacting with our patients to provide care that is responsive to the diverse cultural backgrounds of patients in our highly multicultural nation."

Cultural safety refers to a doctor-patient encounter in which the patient feels respected and empowered, and that their culture and knowledge has been acknowledged. Cultural safety refers to the patient's feelings in the health care encounter, while cultural competence refers to the skills required by a practitioner to ensure that the patient feels safe.

To practice in a manner that is culturally safe, practitioners should reflect on the power differentials inherent in health service delivery. Taking a culturally safe approach also implies acting as a health advocate: working to improve access to care; exposing the social, political, and historical context of health care; and interrupting unequal power relations. Given that the patient exists simultaneously within several caring systems, influenced by their family, community, and traditions, the culturally safe practitioner allows the patient to define what is culturally safe for them.

Our culture influences the way we perceive virtually everything around us, often unconsciously. Several useful concepts describe issues that can arise:

- *Ethnocentrism.* The sense that one's own beliefs, values, and ways of life are superior to, and more desirable than, those of others. For example, you may be trained in Western medicine, but your patient insists on taking a herbal remedy. You may be tempted to say "So, why are you consulting me, then?" Ethnocentrism is often unconscious and implicit in a person's behavior. Personal reflection is a valuable tool for physicians to critically examine their own ethnocentric views and behaviors.

- *Cultural blindness.* This refers to attempts (often well-intentioned) to be unbiased by ignoring the fact of a person's race. It is illustrated in phrases such as "being color blind," or "not seeing race." However, ignoring cultural differences may make people from another culture feel discounted or ignored; what may be transmitted is the impression that race or culture are unimportant, and that values of the dominant culture are universally applicable. Meanwhile, the person who is culturally blind may feel they are being fair and unprejudiced, unaware of how they are making others feel. Cultural blindness becomes, in effect, the opposite of cultural sensitivity.

- *Culture shock.* Most physicians come from middle-class families and have not experienced poverty, homelessness or addictions. Exposure to such realities in their patients therefore requires great adaptations and can be distressing. This is a common experience in those who have visited a slum in a developing country, but may also arise at home in confronting abortion, infanticide, or female circumcision.

- *Cultural conflict.* Conflict generated when the rules of one's own culture are contradicted by the rules of another.
- *Cultural imposition (or cultural assimilation or colonialism).* The imposition of the views and values of your own culture without consideration of the beliefs of others.
- *Stereotyping and generalization.* What may be true of a group need not apply to each individual. Hence, talking about cultures can lead to dangerously prejudicial generalizations. Prejudice is the tendency to use preconceived notions about a group in pre-judging one of the group's members, so applying cultural awareness to individuals can be hazardous. Yet, on the other hand, ignoring culture (cultural blindness) can be equally detrimental. The key is to acknowledge and be respectful of differences, and to ask patients to explain their perspective when in doubt.

The Relevance of Culture for Health

Culture influences health through many channels:

1. *Positive or negative lifestyle behaviors.* While we often focus on the negative influences of lifestyle behavior—such as drug cultures, or the poor diet of some teen cultures, for example— we should not neglect the positive cultural influences on behaviors and practices. For example, Mormons and Seventh Day Adventists have been found to live longer than the general population, in part because of their lifestyle including the avoidance of alcohol and smoking, but also because of enhanced social support.

2. *Health beliefs and attitudes.* These include what a person views as illness that requires treatment, and which treatments and preventive measures he or she will accept, as with the Jehovah's Witness prohibition on using whole blood products.

3. *Reactions to being sick.* A person's adoption of the sick role (and, hence, how he or she or he reacts to being sick) is often guided by his or her cultural roots. For instance,

"machismo" may discourage a man from seeking prompt medical attention, and culture may also influence from whom a person will accept advice.

4. *Communication patterns, including language and modes of thinking.* Beyond these, however, culture may constrain some patients from expressing an opinion to the doctor, or may discourage a wife from speaking freely in front of her husband, for example. Such influences can complicate efforts to establish a therapeutic relationship and, thereby, to help the patient.

5. *Status.* The way in which one culture views another may affect the status of entire groups of people, placing them at a disadvantage. The resulting social inequality or even exclusion forms a health determinant. For example, women in some societies have little power to insist on condom use.

What elements of a patient's culture should a health care provider consider when deciding how best to manage a case?

Cultural influences may affect a patient's reaction to the disease, to suggested therapy, and to efforts to help them prevent recurrences by changing risk factors. Therefore, it may be important for health care providers to find out about such possibilities; they can explain that they need them to tell about their family's and community's feelings about health recommendations. Health care providers should explain that they are not familiar with their community and want them to tell if they may have beliefs or obligations that the health care provider should be aware of, such as any restrictions on diet, medications, etc., if these could be relevant.

Difference Between Cultural Competence and Cultural Safety

Cultural competence is included within cultural safety, but safety goes beyond competence to advocate actively for the patient's perspective, to protect their right to hold the views they do. When a patient knows that you will honor and uphold their perspective and not try to change it, they will be more likely to accept your recommendations. A physician who practices culturally safe care has reflected on her own cultural biases recognizes them and ensures that her biases do not impact the care that the patient receives. This pattern of self-reflection, education and advocacy is also practiced at the organizational level.

Stigmatized Illnesses and Health Care

Being disabled because of a disease or injury can lead to benefits—for example, a parking space that is close by. In some instances, the benefits are very attractive but, in most countries of the world, the disabled have no access to any governmental help, and insurance premiums are so high that only a minority of the population can participate in disability compensations schemes. In some situations, disability due to a war injury or to some other situation that confers hero status can also bring social respect and moral prestige to the disabled person.

For the vast majority of disabled people, however, the disadvantages of disability are much more important than its advantages. A restriction of the possibility of participation in normal social life and limitations in the pursuit of personal happiness are often grave and depressing for the person with an impairment that causes a disability.

When the disease or the situation that has produced impairment is stigmatized, the limitations of functions are aggravated and the possibility of compensating disability is significantly reduced. There are a number of diseases that are stigmatized—mental disorders, AIDS, venereal diseases, leprosy, and certain skin diseases. People who have such diseases are discriminated in the health care system, they usually receive much less social support than those who have non-stigmatizing illnesses and—what is possibly worst—they have grave difficulties in organizing their life if their disease has caused an impairment that can lead to disability and handicaps.

Mental disorders probably carry more stigma (and consequent discrimination) than any other illness. The stigma does not stop at the persons who are suffering from a stigmatized illness. Their immediate and even remote families often experience significant social disadvantages. The institutions that provide mental health care are stigmatized. Stigma reduces the value of the persons who have a mental disorder in the eyes of the community and the government.

Medications that are needed in the treatment of mental disorders, for example, are considered expensive even when their cost is much lower than the cost of drugs used in the treatment of other illnesses: they are not considered expensive because of their cost but because they are meant to be used in the treatment of people who are not considered to be of much value to the society.

The awareness of the fact that stigmatization is one of the major—if not the major—obstacles to the improvement of care for people with stigmatized illnesses is gradually growing. In a number of countries governments, non-governmental organizations, and health institutions have launched campaigns to reduce stigma related to illness. They display posters and distribute leaflets, as well as organize radio and television programs.

There is, however, an important sector employing many individuals that does not participate very actively in the reduction of stigma and in efforts to eliminate the discrimination that follows it. It is the health sector—which, by its definition, could gain from the reduction of stigma almost as much as the individuals who have the stigmatized illness. The managements of general hospitals, as well as heads of various medical departments often refuse to have a department of psychiatry and, if they accept it, they usually assign the worst accommodation for it—in a remote corner of the hospital grounds, for example, or in the lowest (sometimes partly underground) floor. In the order of priority for maintenance or renovation work departments of psychiatry come last although they are often in a pitiful state. Doctors who are not involved in mental health care participate and sometimes excel in making fun of the mentally ill, of psychiatrists, and of mental illness. They will often refuse to deal with physical illness in a person with a mental disorder and send such patients to their psychiatrist, although they are better placed to deal with the physical illness than the psychiatrist.

Nor are the psychiatrists and other mental health care staff doing as much as they should about the reduction of stigma. They seem unaware of the stigmatizing effects of their use of language—they speak of schizophrenics when they should say a person with schizophrenia and about misbehavior or lack of discipline when they should make it clear that behavioral abnormalities are part of the illness they are supposed to recognize and treat. In some countries they requested and received longer holidays or somewhat higher salaries saying that they deserve this because they deal with dangerous patients—although they have publicly proclaimed that mental illness is a disease like any other. They often disregard complaints about the physical health of people with mental disorders and do not do much about them, thus providing sub-optimal care and contributing to the tendency to dismiss whatever people with mental illness may be saying. In their teaching activities, stigmatization as well as the prevention of discrimination and its other consequences often receive only minimal attention.

Perhaps it is impossible for the health care workers themselves to launch large anti-stigma programs: what, however, they should and can do is to examine their own behavior and activity to ensure that they do not contribute to stigmatization and consequent discrimination. They should also participate in the efforts of others to reduce stigma or initiate such efforts whenever possible. Doing nothing about stigma and discrimination that follows it is no longer an acceptable option.

The Cultural Meaning of Illness

Our culture, not our biology, dictates which illnesses are stigmatized and which are not, which are considered disabilities and which are not, and which are deemed contestable (meaning some medical professionals may find the existence of this ailment questionable) as opposed to definitive (illnesses that are unquestionably recognized in the medical profession). For instance, sociologist Erving Goffman described how social stigmas hinder individuals from fully integrating into society. The stigmatization of illness often has the greatest effect on the patient and the kind of care he or she receives. Many contend that our society and even our health care institutions discriminate against certain diseases—like mental disorders, AIDS, venereal diseases, and skin disorders. Facilities for these diseases may be sub-par; they may be segregated from other health care areas or relegated to a poorer environment. The stigma may keep people from seeking help for their illness, making it worse than it needs to be. Contested illnesses are those that are questioned or questionable by some medical professionals. Disorders like fibromyalgia or chronic fatigue syndrome may be either true illnesses or only in the patients' heads, depending on the opinion of the medical professional. This dynamic can affect how a patient seeks treatment and what kind of treatment he or she receives.

In terms of constructing the illness experience, culture and individual personality both play a significant role. For some people, a long-term illness can have the effect of making their world smaller, more defined by the illness than anything else. For others, illness can be a chance for discovery, for re-imaging a new self (Conrad and Barker 2007). Culture plays a huge role in how an individual experiences illness. Widespread diseases like AIDS or breast cancer have specific cultural markers that have changed over the years and that govern how individuals—and society—view them.

Today, many institutions of wellness acknowledge the degree to which individual perceptions shape the nature of health and illness. Regarding physical activity, for instance, the Centers for Disease Control (CDC) recommends that individuals use a standard level of exertion to assess their physical activity. This Rating of Perceived Exertion (RPE) gives a more complete view of an individual's actual exertion level, since heart-rate or pulse measurements may be affected by medication or other issues. Similarly, many medical professionals use a comparable scale for perceived pain to help determine pain management strategies.

Subtle Differences in Language Affect How People with Mental Illnesses Are Viewed

Rick Nauert

Rick Nauert is an associate news editor with Psych Central. *He is also an associate professor at Rocky Mountain University of Health Professionals in their doctoral program in health promotion and wellness.*

New research suggests even subtle differences in how you refer to people with mental illness can affect levels of tolerance.

In a first-of-its-kind study, researchers found that participants showed less tolerance toward people who were referred to as "the mentally ill" when compared to those referred to as "people with mental illness."

Ohio State investigators discovered participants were more likely to agree with the statement "the mentally ill should be isolated from the community" than the almost identical statement "people with mental illnesses should be isolated from the community."

These results were found among college students and non-student adults and even professional counselors who took part in the study.

The findings suggest that language choice should not be viewed just as an issue of "political correctness," said Darcy Haag Granello, Ph.D., co-author of the study and a professor of educational studies.

"This isn't just about saying the right thing for appearances," she said. "The language we use has real effects on our levels of tolerance for people with mental illness."

Granello conducted the study with Todd Gibbs, a graduate student in educational studies at Ohio State. Their results appear in *The Journal of Counseling and Development.*

"Language Matters When Referring to Mental Illness," by Rick Nauert, PhD, Psych Central, August 8, 2018. Reprinted by permission.

The push to change how society refers to people with mental illness began in the 1990s when several professional publications proposed the use of what they called "person-first" language when talking about people with disabilities or chronic conditions.

"Person-first language is a way to honor the personhood of an individual by separating their identity from any disability or diagnosis he or she might have," Gibbs said.

"When you say 'people with a mental illness,' you are emphasizing that they aren't defined solely by their disability. But when you talk about 'the mentally ill' the disability is the entire definition of the person," he said.

Although the use of person-first language was first proposed more than 20 years ago, this is the first study examining how the use of such language could affect tolerance toward people with mental illness, Granello said.

"It is shocking to me that there hasn't been research on this before. It is such a simple study. But the results show that our intuition about the importance of person-first language was valid."

The research involved three groups of people: 221 undergraduate students, 211 non-student adults, and 269 professional counselors and counselors-in-training who were attending a meeting of the American Counseling Association.

The design of the study was very simple. All participants completed a standard, often-used survey instrument created in 1979 called the Community Attitudes Toward the Mentally Ill.

The CAMI is a 40-item survey designed to measure people's attitudes toward people with diagnosable mental illness. Participants indicated the degree to which they agreed with the statements on a five-point scale from one (strongly disagree) to five (strongly agree).

The questionnaires were identical in all ways except one: Half the people received a survey where all references were to "the mentally ill" and half received a survey where all references were to "people with mental illnesses."

The questionnaires had four subscales looking at different aspects of how people view those with mental illnesses. The four subscales (and sample questions) are:

- Authoritarianism: "The mentally ill (or "People with mental illness") need the same kind of control and discipline as a young child."
- Benevolence: "The mentally ill (or "People with mental illness") have for too long been the subject of ridicule."
- Social restrictiveness: "The mentally ill (or "People with mental illness") should be isolated from the rest of the community."
- Community mental health ideology: "Having the mentally ill (or "people with mental illness") living within residential neighborhoods might be good therapy, but the risks to residents are too great."

Investigators discovered that each of the three groups studied (college students, other adults, counselors) showed less tolerance when their surveys referred to "the mentally ill," but in slightly different ways.

College students showed less tolerance on the authoritarianism and social restrictiveness scales; other adults showed less tolerance on benevolence and community mental health ideology subscales; and counselors and counselors-in-training showed less tolerance on the authoritarianism and social restrictiveness subscales.

Nevertheless, Granello explains that since the study was only exploratory, it is too early to draw conclusions about the differences in how each group responded on the four subscales.

"The important point to take away is that no one, at least in our study, was immune," Granello said. "All showed some evidence of being affected by the language used to describe people with mental illness."

One surprising finding was that the counselors—although they showed more tolerance overall than the other two groups—

showed the largest difference in tolerance levels depending on the language they read.

"Even counselors who work every day with people who have mental illness can be affected by language. They need to be aware of how language might influence their decision-making when they work with clients," she said.

Granello said the overall message of the study is that everyone, including the media, policymakers and the general public, needs to change how they refer to people with mental illness.

"I understand why people use the term 'the mentally ill.' It is shorter and less cumbersome than saying 'people with mental illness,'" she said.

"But I think people with mental illness deserve to have us change our language. Even if it is more awkward for us, it helps change our perception, which ultimately may lead us to treat all people with the respect and understanding they deserve."

People with Mental Illness Face Widespread Stereotypes

Judy Baker

Judy Baker is a dean at Foothill College in Los Altos Hills, California. She earned her doctorate in health education from the University of Texas and her master's degree in social work from Virginia Commonwealth University. She has taught a variety of community health courses at both the graduate and undergraduate level.

Words can hurt. Many derogatory words and phrases are used in relation to mental illness. However, these words maintain the stereotyped image and not the reality about mental illness. Try not to use these words, and encourage students not to use them. It is more appropriate to refer to "a person who has a mental illness" when speaking about someone.

"Mentally ill people are nuts, crazy, wacko." "Mentally ill people are morally bad." "Mentally ill people are dangerous and should be locked in an asylum forever." "Mentally ill people need somebody to take care of them." How often have we heard comments like these or seen these types of portrayals in movies, television shows, or books? We may even be guilty of making comments like them ourselves. Is there any truth behind these portrayals, or is that negative view based on our ignorance and fear?

Stigmas are negative stereotypes about groups of people. Common stigmas about people who are mentally ill are:

- Individuals who have a mental illness are dangerous.
- Individuals who have a mental illness are irresponsible and can't make life decisions for themselves.

- People who have a mental illness are childlike and must be taken care of by parents or guardians.
- People who have a mental illness should just get over it.

Each of those preconceptions about people who have a mental illness is based on false information. Very few people who have a mental illness are dangerous to society. Most can hold jobs, attend school, and live independently. A person who has a mental illness cannot simply decide to get over it any more than someone who has a different chronic disease such as diabetes, asthma, or heart disease can. A mental illness, like those other diseases, is caused by a physical problem in the body.

Stigmas against individuals who have a mental illness lead to injustices, including discriminatory decisions regarding housing, employment, and education. Overcoming the stigmas commonly associated with mental illness is yet one more challenge that people who have a mental illness must face. Indeed, many people who successfully manage their mental illness report that the stigma they face is in many ways more disabling than the illness itself. The stigmatizing attitudes toward mental illness held by both the public and those who have a mental illness lead to feelings of shame and guilt, loss of self-esteem, social dependence, and a sense of isolation and hopelessness. One of the worst consequences of stigma is that people who are struggling with a mental illness may be reluctant to seek treatment that, in most cases, would significantly relieve their symptoms.

Providing accurate information is one way to reduce stigmas about mental illness. Advocacy groups protest stereotypes imposed upon those who are mentally ill. They demand that the media stop presenting inaccurate views of mental illness and that the public stops believing these negative views. A powerful way of countering stereotypes about mental illness occurs when members of the public meet people who are effectively managing a serious mental illness: holding jobs, providing for themselves, and living as good neighbors in a community. Interaction with people who have mental illnesses challenges a person's assumptions and changes a person's attitudes about mental illness.

Stigma and Illness

Stigma has been defined as an attribute that is deeply discrediting. This stigmatized trait sets the bearer apart from the rest of society, bringing with it feelings of shame and isolation. Often, when a person with a stigmatized trait is unable to perform an action because of the condition, other people view the person as the problem rather than viewing the condition as the problem. More recent definitions of stigma focus on the results of stigma—the prejudice, avoidance, rejection and discrimination directed at people believed to have an illness, disorder or other trait perceived to be undesirable. Stigma causes needless suffering, potentially causing a person to deny symptoms, delay treatment and refrain from daily activities. Stigma can exclude people from access to housing, employment, insurance, and appropriate medical care. Thus, stigma can interfere with prevention efforts, and examining and combating stigma is a public health priority.

The Substance Abuse and Mental Health Services Administration (SAMHSA) and the CDC have examined public attitudes toward mental illness in two surveys. In the 2006 HealthStyles survey, only one-quarter of young adults between the ages of 18–24 believed that a person with mental illness can eventually recover. In 2007, adults in 37 states and territories were surveyed about their attitudes toward mental illness, using the 2007 Behavioral Risk Factor Surveillance System Mental Illness and Stigma module. This study found that:

- 78% of adults with mental health symptoms and 89% of adults without such symptoms agreed that treatment can help persons with mental illness lead normal lives.
- 57% of adults without mental health symptoms believed that people are caring and sympathetic to persons with mental illness.

- Only 25% of adults with mental health symptoms believed that people are caring and sympathetic to persons with mental illness.

These findings highlight both the need to educate the public about how to support persons with mental illness and the need to reduce barriers for those seeking or receiving treatment for mental illness.

Challenging Stereotypes About Mental Illness

Recovery from mental illness is a complex process. As with all serious illness, the well-being of recovering individuals is affected by the attitudes that surround them. Despite increasing sensitivity about most disabilities, mental illness all too often remains a target for ridicule and misrepresentation in advertising, entertainment, and the mainstream media.

Most of what we know as individuals comes not from personal experience, but from the stories that surround us from birth. In the past it was families, religious institutions, schools, and respected members of the community who instilled cultural attitudes. "Today, this is done by the mass media," says George Gerbner, founder of the Cultural Environment Movement, and a researcher whose career includes 30 years of monitoring the cultural impact of television on society. Television is, in Gerbner's words, "the wholesale distributor of the stigma of mental illness." His research has shown that characters portrayed on television as having mental illnesses have four times the violence rate and six times the victimization rate of other characters. Gerbner notes that "Violence and retribution are shown as inherent in the illness itself and thus inescapable. No other group in the dramatic world of television suffers and is shown to deserve such a dire fate."

The portrayal of mental illness in the movies is similarly distorted. In the late 1980s, Steven E. Hyler of Columbia University and his colleagues identified six categories of psychiatric characters in films: homicidal maniac, narcissistic parasite, seductress, enlightened member of society, rebellious free spirit, and zoo specimen. Hyler concluded that these predominantly negative stereotypes had a damaging effect on the viewing public and on the patients themselves, their family members, and policy makers. More recently, Otto F. Wahl of George Mason University, an authority on public images of mental illness, found that in the decade from 1985 to 1995, Hollywood released more than 150 films with characters who have mental illnesses, the majority of them killers and villains. There can be no doubt that Hollywood stereotypes are a large part of what people know, or think they know, about people with psychiatric vulnerabilities. Newspaper reports about mental illness are often more accurate than the characters one sees in TV entertainment and movies. Still, people with psychiatric histories generally are reported negatively. In 1991, researchers Russell E. Shain and Julie Phillips, using the United Press International database from 1983, found that 86 percent of all print stories dealing with former mental patients focused on violent crime. A 1997 British study found similarly skewed stories, and a 1999 German study concludes that selective reporting about mental illness causes audiences to distort their view of the "real world." Media stereotypes of persons with mental illness as villains, failures, buffoons—together with the misuse of terms like "schizophrenia" and "psychotic" in negative contexts—have far-reaching consequences. On the most deeply personal level, biased stereotypes damage the sense of self-worth of millions of persons diagnosed with serious psychiatric illnesses. On the social and economic levels, negative stereotyping may result in large-scale discrimination against an entire class of people in the areas of housing, employment, health insurance, and medical treatment.

[...]

The Roots of Stigma

Stigmatization of people with mental disorders has persisted throughout history. It is manifested by bias, distrust, stereotyping, fear, embarrassment, anger, and/or avoidance. Stigma leads others to avoid living, socializing or working with, renting to, or employing people with mental disorders, especially severe disorders such as schizophrenia. It reduces patients' access to resources and opportunities (e.g., housing, jobs) and leads to low self-esteem, isolation, and hopelessness. It deters the public from seeking, and wanting to pay for, care. In its most overt and egregious form, stigma results in outright discrimination and abuse. More tragically, it deprives people of their dignity and interferes with their full participation in society.

Explanations for stigma stem, in part, from the misguided split between mind and body first proposed by Descartes. Another source of stigma lies in the 19th-century separation of the mental health treatment system in the United States from the mainstream of health. These historical influences exert an often immediate influence on perceptions and behaviors in the modern world.

Public Attitudes About Mental Illness: 1950s to 1990s

Nationally representative surveys have tracked public attitudes about mental illness since the 1950s. To permit comparisons over time, several surveys of the 1970s and the 1990s phrased questions exactly as they had been asked in the 1950s.

In the 1950s, the public viewed mental illness as a stigmatized condition and displayed an unscientific understanding of mental illness. Survey respondents typically were not able to identify individuals as "mentally ill" when presented with vignettes of individuals who would have been said to be mentally ill according to the professional standards of the day. The public was not particularly skilled at distinguishing mental illness from ordinary unhappiness and worry and tended to see only extreme forms of behavior—namely psychosis—as mental illness. Mental illness carried great social stigma, especially linked with fear of unpredictable and violent behavior.

By 1996, a modern survey revealed that Americans had achieved greater scientific understanding of mental illness. But the increases in knowledge did not defuse social stigma. The public learned to define mental illness and to distinguish it from ordinary worry and unhappiness. It expanded its definition of mental illness to encompass anxiety, depression, and other mental disorders. The public attributed mental illness to a mix of biological abnormalities and vulnerabilities to social and psychological stress. Yet, in comparison with the 1950s, the public's perception of mental illness more frequently incorporated violent behavior. This was primarily true among those who defined mental illness to include psychosis (a view held by about one-third of the entire sample). Thirty-one percent of this group mentioned violence in its descriptions of mental illness, in comparison with 13 percent in the 1950s. In other words, the perception of people with psychosis as being dangerous is stronger today than in the past.

The 1996 survey also probed how perceptions of those with mental illness varied by diagnosis. The public was more likely to consider an individual with schizophrenia as having mental illness than an individual with depression. All of them were distinguished reasonably well from a worried and unhappy individual who did not meet professional criteria for a mental disorder. The desire for social distance was consistent with this hierarchy.

[...]

Stigma and Seeking Help for Mental Disorders

Nearly two-thirds of all people with diagnosable mental disorders do not seek treatment. Stigma surrounding the receipt of mental health treatment is among the many barriers that discourage people from seeking treatment. Concern about stigma appears to be heightened in rural areas in relation to larger towns or cities. Stigma also disproportionately affects certain age groups, as explained in the chapters on children and older people.

The surveys cited above concerning evolving public attitudes about mental illness also monitored how people would cope with, and seek treatment for, mental illness if they became symptomatic. (The term "nervous breakdown" was used in lieu of the term "mental illness" in the 1996 survey to allow for comparisons with the surveys in the 1950s and 1970s.) The 1996 survey found that people were likelier than in the past to approach mental illness by coping with, rather than by avoiding, the problem. They also were more likely now to want informal social supports (e.g., self-help groups). Those who now sought formal support increasingly preferred counselors, psychologists, and social workers.

Stigma and Paying for Mental Disorder Treatment

Another manifestation of stigma is reflected in the public's reluctance to pay for mental health services. Public willingness to pay for mental health treatment, particularly through insurance premiums or taxes, has been assessed largely through public opinion polls. Members of the public report a greater willingness to pay for insurance coverage for individuals with severe mental disorders, such as schizophrenia and depression, rather than for less severe conditions such as worry and unhappiness. While the public generally appears to support paying for treatment, its support diminishes upon the realization that higher taxes or premiums would be necessary. In the lexicon of survey research, the willingness to pay for mental illness treatment services is considered to be "soft." The public generally ranks insurance coverage for mental disorders below that for somatic disorders.

Reducing Stigma

There is likely no simple or single panacea to eliminate the stigma associated with mental illness. Stigma was expected to abate with increased knowledge of mental illness, but just the opposite occurred: stigma in some ways intensified over the past 40 years even though understanding improved. Knowledge of mental illness appears by itself insufficient to dispel stigma. Broader knowledge may be warranted, especially to redress public fears. Research is beginning to demonstrate that negative perceptions about severe mental illness can be lowered by furnishing empirically based information on the association between violence and severe mental illness. Overall approaches to stigma reduction involve programs of advocacy, public education, and contact with persons with mental illness through schools and other societal institutions.

Ironically, these examples also illustrate a more unsettling consequence: that the mental health field was adversely affected when causes and treatments were identified. As advances were achieved, each condition was transferred from the mental health field to another medical specialty. For instance, dominion over syphilis was moved to dermatology, internal medicine, and neurology upon advances in etiology and treatment. Dominion over hormone-related mental disorders was moved to endocrinology under similar circumstances. The consequence of this transformation, according to historian Gerald Grob, is that the mental health field became over the years the repository for mental disorders whose etiology was unknown. This left the mental health field "vulnerable to accusations by their medical brethren that psychiatry was not part of medicine, and that psychiatric practice rested on superstition and myth."

These historical examples signify that stigma dissipates for individual disorders once advances render them less disabling, infectious, or disfiguring. Yet the stigma surrounding other mental disorders not only persists but may be inadvertently reinforced by leaving to mental health care only those behavioral conditions without known causes or cures. To point this out is not intended to imply that advances in mental health should be halted; rather, advances should be nurtured and heralded. The purpose here is to explain some of the historical origins of the chasm between the health and mental health fields.

[…]

Violence and Mental Illness: The Facts

The discrimination and stigma associated with mental illnesses largely stem from the link between mental illness and violence in the minds of the general public, according to the US Surgeon General. The belief that persons with mental illness are dangerous is a significant factor in the development of stigma and discrimination. The effects of stigma and discrimination are profound. The President's New Freedom Commission on Mental Health found that, "Stigma leads others to avoid living, socializing, or working with, renting to, or employing people with mental disorders—especially severe disorders, such as schizophrenia. It leads to low self-esteem, isolation, and hopelessness. It deters the public from seeking and wanting to pay for care. Responding to stigma, people with mental health problems internalize public attitudes and become so embarrassed or ashamed that they often conceal symptoms and fail to seek treatment."

This link is often promoted by the entertainment and news media. For example, Mental Health America, (formerly the National Mental Health Association) reported that, according to a survey for the Screen Actors' Guild, characters in prime time television portrayed as having a mental illness are depicted as the most dangerous of all demographic groups: 60 percent were shown to be involved in crime or violence. Also most news accounts portray people with mental illness as dangerous. The vast majority of news stories on mental illness either focus on other negative characteristics related to people with the disorder (e.g., unpredictability and unsociability) or on medical treatments. Notably absent are positive stories that highlight recovery of many persons with even the most serious of mental illnesses. Inaccurate and stereotypical representations of mental illness also exist in other mass media, such as films, music, novels and cartoons.

Most citizens believe persons with mental illnesses are dangerous. A longitudinal study of Americans' attitudes on mental health between 1950 and 1996 found, "the proportion of Americans who describe mental illness in terms consistent with violent or dangerous behavior nearly doubled." Also, the vast majority of Americans believe that persons with mental illnesses pose a threat for violence towards others and themselves.

As a result, Americans are hesitant to interact with people who have mental illnesses. Thirty-eight percent are unwilling to be friends with someone having mental health difficulties; sixty-four percent do not want someone who has schizophrenia as a close co-worker, and more than sixty-eight percent are unwilling to have someone with depression marry into their family.

But, in truth, people have little reason for such fears.

[...]

For people with mental illnesses, violent behavior appears to be more common when there's also the presence of other risk factors. These include substance abuse or dependence; a history of violence, juvenile detention, or physical abuse; and recent stressors such as being a crime victim, getting divorced, or losing a job.

In addition:

- "Research has shown that the vast majority of people who are violent do not suffer from mental illnesses" (American Psychiatric Association, 1994).
- "... [T]he absolute risk of violence among the mentally ill as a group is still very small and . . . only a small proportion of the violence in our society can be attributed to persons who are mentally ill" (Mulvey, 1994).
- In a 1998 study that compared people discharged from acute psychiatric inpatient facilities and others in the same neighborhoods, researchers found that "there was no significant difference between the prevalence of violence by patients without symptoms of substance abuse and the prevalence of violence by others living in the same neighborhoods who were also without symptoms of substance abuse" (Steadman, Mulvey, Monahan, Robbins, Applebaum, Grisso, Roth, and Silver, 1998).

People with psychiatric disabilities are far more likely to be victims than perpetrators of violent crime. Researchers at North Carolina State University and Duke University found that people with severe mental illnesses—schizophrenia, bipolar disorder or psychosis—are 2 ½ times more likely to be attacked, raped or mugged than the general population.

People with mental illnesses can and do recover. People with mental illnesses can recover or manage their conditions and go on to lead happy, healthy, productive lives. They contribute to society and make the world a better place. People can often benefit from medication, rehabilitation, talk therapy, self help or a combination of these. One of the most important factors in recovery is the understanding and acceptance of family and friends.

The Media Is Mostly to Blame for Perpetuating Stigma About Mental Illness

Naveed Saleh

Naveed Saleh is a doctor, author, science writer, and editor based in Southern California. He is a long-time blogger at Psychology Today *and has written for various online and print publications as well.*

I n the aftermath of an unconscionable act of random violence, many people are inclined to label the perpetrator "crazy." Although the criminal may have a mental illness, automatically assigning the label "crazy" does a great disservice to people who live with mental illness every day.

In reality, somebody with mental illness is much more likely to be a victim—rather than a perpetrator—of violence. Calling a violent offender "crazy" spreads a dangerous stereotype and belies the complex relationship between criminality and mental illness.

The media teaches us about people with whom we do not routinely interact. This constant flow of data gives us incessant social cues about the nature of other groups of people—including which groups of people should be praised or scorned.

Media portrayals of those with mental illness often skew toward either stigmatization or trivialization. Consequently, all forms of media—including television, film, magazines, newspapers, and social media—have been roundly criticized for disseminating negative stereotypes and inaccurate descriptions of those with mental illness.

What Is Stigmatization

Stigma happens when some person is viewed as an "other." This other is denied full social acceptance.

"How the Stigma of Mental Health Is Spread by Mass Media," by Naveed Saleh, MD, MS, Dotdash Publishing, December 3, 2018. Reprinted by permission.

Here is how stigma is defined by Brian K. Ahmedani in a 2011 article titled "Mental Health Stigma: Society, Individuals, and the Profession":

> The most established definition regarding stigma is written by Erving Goffman (1963) in his seminal work: *Stigma: Notes on the Management of Spoiled Identity*. Goffman states that stigma is "an attribute that is deeply discrediting" that reduces someone "from a whole and usual person to a tainted, discounted one" (p. 3). The stigmatized, thus, are perceived as having a "spoiled identity" (Goffman, 1963, p. 3). In the social work literature, Dudley, working from Goffman's initial conceptualization, defined stigma as stereotypes or negative views attributed to a person or groups of people when their characteristics or behaviors are viewed as different from or inferior to societal norms.

Of note, stigmatization is so entwined with the media that researchers have used newspaper articles as a proxy metric for stigma in society.

Stigmatization of Mental Illness By the Media

Let's consider some stigmatizations of mental illness disseminated by the media as hypothesized by Jessica Gall Myrick and Rachelle Pavelko in a 2017 article published in the *Journal of Health Communication*.

First, mental illnesses such as schizophrenia are seen as so disruptive to society than those with such conditions must be isolated from society altogether.

Second, media accounts focus on the individual with mental illness rather than framing mental illness as a societal issue. Consequently, media consumers are more likely to blame the individual for the illness.

Third, people with mental illness suffer from overgeneralization in media portrayals; everybody with a specific condition is expected to portray the same characteristics of the disease. For instance, depictions that all people with depression are suicidal, and all people with schizophrenia hallucinate. (In reality, only between

60 and 80 percent of people with schizophrenia experience auditory hallucinations, and a smaller number experience visual hallucinations.)

Fourth, media portrayals discount the fact that many people with mental illness don't need to disclose this condition to everyone around them. Instead—whether by intention or not—mental illness often goes unrecognized. Portrayals in the media, however, present situations where everyone knows about a character's mental illness, and this mental illness is no longer concealed.

Fifth, the media portrays mental illness as being untreatable or unrecoverable.

Trivialization of Mental Illness By the Media

"Trivialization suggests the opposite in the case of mediated representations of mental illness: a downplaying of the notability or negativity of these conditions," write Myrick and Pavelko.

Here are some possible ways that trivialization can rear its head in the media.

First, the media promotes mental illness as either not being severe or being less severe than it really is. For instance, many people with anorexia feel like their condition is made out to be less severe than it really is—in part because people with the condition who are portrayed in the media minimize it's serious and hide severe consequences.

In reality, the death rate of anorexia is the highest death rate of an eating disorder. In an oft-cited meta-analysis published in *JAMA Psychiatry* in 2011, Jon Arcelus and colleagues analyzed 36 studies representing 17,272 individual patients with eating disorders and found that 755 died.

Second, mental illness is oversimplified in the media. For instance, people with OCD are depicted as being overly concerned with cleanliness and perfectionism. However, the obsessive thoughts that drive these compulsions are overlooked.

Third, the symptoms of mental illness are portrayed in the media as beneficial. For example, in the television series *Monk*, the protagonist is a detective who has OCD and pays close attention to detail, which helps him solve the crime and advance his career.

Alternatively, there's the "super-cripple" misrepresentation. According to Myrick and Pavelko: "Akin to a mental ailment being perceived as an advantage, individuals with physical ailments have also been associated with the 'super cripple' label, a stereotype that attributes magical, superhuman traits to people with disabilities."

Fourth, using media channels, people without disabilities mock people with disabilities by appropriating mental-illness terminology. For instance, the hashtag OCD (#OCD) is commonly used on Twitter to describe attention to cleanliness or organization.

Depictions of Schizophrenia in Film

Probably the most disparaging stigmatizations of mental illness in media lie in the film portrayals of antagonists with mental illness. In particular, characters with schizophrenia are presented as "homicidal maniacs" in "slasher" or "psycho killer" movies.

Such portrayals disseminate misinformation about the symptoms, causes, and treatment of people with schizophrenia and other forms of severe mental illness. Of note, popular movies have been shown to exert potent influences on attitude formation.

In a 2012 article titled the "Portrayals of Schizophrenia by Entertainment Media: A Content Analysis of Contemporary Movies," Patricia R. Owen analyzed 41 movies released between 1990 and 2010 for depictions of schizophrenia and found the following:

Most characters displayed positive symptoms of schizophrenia. Delusions were featured most frequently, followed by auditory and visual hallucinations. A majority of characters displayed violent behavior toward themselves or others and nearly one-third of violent characters engaged in homicidal behavior. About one-fourth of characters committed suicide. Causation of schizophrenia was infrequently noted, although about one-fourth of movies implied that a traumatic life event was significant in causation. Of movies alluding to or showing treatment, psychotropic medications were most commonly portrayed.

These portrayals were wrong and damaging for several reasons, including the following:

1. Portrayals of schizophrenia in recent movies often focused on the positive symptoms of the disease, such as visual hallucinations, bizarre delusions, and disorganized speech. These symptoms were presented as commonplace when, in fact, negative symptoms, such as poverty of speech, decreased motivation, and flat affect, are more common.

2. Several movies spread the false stereotype that people with schizophrenia are prone to violence and unpredictable behavior. Moreover, some movies presented people with schizophrenia as being "possessed." These violent stereotypes poison viewers and engender harsh negative attitudes toward mental illness.

3. In these movies, 24 percent of the characters with schizophrenia committed suicide, which is misleading because in reality only between 10 percent and 16 percent of people with schizophrenia commit suicide during the course of a lifetime.

4. Characters with schizophrenia were usually depicted as white males. In reality, schizophrenia disproportionately affects African Americans. Furthermore, schizophrenia affects men and women almost equally.

5. In a few movies, schizophrenia is depicted as secondary to traumatic life events or   curable by love, which are both misrepresentations of the disease.

On the bright side, Owen found that not all the information presented about schizophrenia in the modern film was stigmatizing. For example, in more than half of the movies analyzed, the use of psychiatric medications was depicted or alluded to. Furthermore, nearly half the characters with schizophrenia were depicted as poor, which jells with the epidemiological data that suggest people of higher socioeconomic means are less likely to experience schizophrenia.

Ultimately, negative portrayals—especially violent negative portrayals—of people with schizophrenia and other severe types of mental illness in the media contribute to stigmatization, stereotyping, discrimination, and social rejection.

What Can Be Done About the Stigma of Mental Health

In their 2017 study, Myrick and Pavelko found that television, movies, and social media are the most frequent sources of portrayals of mental illness that stigmatize and trivialize.

However, as noted by the authors: "Given the power of media to quickly and widely spread inaccurate portrayals, a deeper understanding of their similarities, differences, and interactive effects is called for."

We still need to better understand how these messages are disseminated by the media before we can act to rectify them. Currently, there is limited research examining how the media promotes mental-illness stereotypes, stigmatization, and trivialization. Nevertheless, certain suggestions regarding how to improve the depiction of those with mental illness in the media have been made.

1. Analyze mass-media production procedures to better understand the current practices, needs, values, and economic realities of screenwriters, producers, and journalists. For instance, understanding the balance between being newsworthy or emotionally arousing and verifiable.
2. Present mental illness only when relevant to the story.
3. Prefer non-individualized descriptions of mental illness and instead focus on the societal aspects.
4. Include expert input from psychiatrists during production.
5. Implement a mental health short course when training journalists.

6. Use mental-health terminology with precision, fairness, and expertise.

As individuals who consume copious amounts of mass media and engage on social media routinely, the best thing that we can do is to stop using words like "crazy" and "deranged" in a derogatory or flippant fashion. Moreover, it's best not to make psychiatric diagnoses outside of a clinical setting. Only a specialist can make a diagnosis of OCD, depression, bipolar disorder, schizophrenia, and so forth. By labeling without proof, we hurt those who really live with mental illness on a daily basis.

Young People with Mental Illness Aren't Ashamed to Admit It

Iran Daily

The Iran Daily *is an English-language publication from the Islamic Republic News Agency. It covers global news, politics, sports, and other topics.*

As Indiana University of Pennsylvania's Council of Trustees learned during a Student Affairs Committee presentation, more students are seeking mental health care services.

"We have seen an absolute explosion," said Dr. Jessica Miller, director of Indiana University of Pennsylvania (IUP)'s Counseling Center.

According to indianagazette.com, the university's Health Services reported seeing 122 patients with a mental health diagnosis this fall, compared with 56 in the fall of 2017, 54 in the fall of 2016 and 39 in the fall of 2015.

And Dr. Charles J. Fey, interim vice president for student affairs, said there was an increase for a seventh straight year in the number of students most concerned about a "threat to self."

Miller and other IUP officials told the committee that it is part of a nationwide trend.

According to an October report quoted by the health care-oriented WebMD, anxiety, depression and panic attacks are sending college students in the United States to mental health clinics in record numbers.

Between 2009 and 2015, the HealthDay News report on the WebMD website said, treatment and diagnoses of anxiety increased by nearly six percent among these students, followed by depression and panic attacks, which each increased about three percent.

Researchers led by Sara Oswalt, chairwoman of the Department of Kinesiology, Health and Nutrition at the University of Texas at San Antonio, found anxiety is the most common problem, affecting almost 15 percent of college students across the nation.

HealthDay News reported that Oswalt and her colleagues used data from the American College Health Association to collect information on more than 450,000 undergraduates.

It's not clear if the college environment is causing or even contributing to the increase in these problems, Oswalt told HealthDay News, but if mental health problems aren't addressed, success in school is jeopardized.

IUP officials could offer evidence of that, telling the Student Affairs Committee of an 0.4-point decline in the grade point average among students with anxiety and mild to severe depression.

And it is part of an overall increase in the number of students seeking medical assistance, at a university that can provide care to 100 or more students each day.

Director of Health Services Melissa Dick said 5,619 students utilized Health Services in the past year, compared to 5,568 five years ago—when IUP had far more students, 14,369 then to 11,325 this fall.

Miller said various factors are driving the demand for additional mental health services, including a reduced stigma about seeking such care.

"Students are much more open to seeking services," Miller said.

In fact, they've been so open that there's a backlog, with 55 students on a waitlist for appointments at mid-semester.

That's despite things the university is doing, such as moving to a triage model to assess students on the same day and having walk-in hours Monday through Friday between 1 and 3 p.m. at the health center in the Suites on Maple East.

A clinical case manager has been added as well to expedite local referrals and enroll eligible students in medical assistance.

Miller also illustrated factors contributing to the increase, including substance abuse, social media, intensified expectations, new parenting styles and the political climate.

Miller said so far this year there have been 25 calls from parents expressing concern about their children at IUP.

Also addressing the Student Affairs Committee were Drs. Dan Burkett and Sondra Dennison, co-conveners of the Concern and Response Team, where IUP students, faculty, and staff can seek advice about a student's observed behaviors.

They said collaboration across the university community to implement effective intervention is essential to ensuring student success and retention.

Efforts Are Being Made to Improve the National Conversation About Suicide

Sally Spencer-Thomas

Dr. Sally Spencer-Thomas is a clinical psychologist who writes the employee well-being column for IRMI.com. She received a doctorate in clinical psychology from the University of Denver and focuses on mental health advocacy and suicide prevention.

Whenever a celebrity dies by suicide, the world pays attention, and the suicide prevention community braces for impact. Why? We know that the media will often circulate unsafe messaging for days after the tragedies and that this will have a suicide exposure effect on many people who are already vulnerable to suicide.

Recently, we lost not one but two well-known celebrities to suicide. Immediately, major media outlets went into high gear. Some journalists—unknowingly or intentionally—have been reporting in a way that has been shown in the research to increase suicide risk. Many elements of their reporting—romanticizing, glamorizing, gratuitously detailing the means of death, or depicting the death scene—are considered unsafe reporting practices and have been shown to contribute to an uptick in suicide attempts and deaths in the days and weeks following a celebrity's suicide. Several other media outlets did an outstanding job reporting these newsworthy events with sensitivity and followed practices that would help people find hope and link to life-saving resources like the National Suicide Prevention Lifeline.

Decades of research summarized in the Suicide Prevention Resource Center safe messaging reference guide encourage those who are giving public communications about suicide to follow these suggestions.[1]

- Portray help-seeking as a reasonable action.

"Language Matters: Why We Don't Say 'Committed Suicide,'" by Sally Spencer-Thomas, International Risk Management Institute, Inc., June 2018. Reprinted by permission.

- Provide resources to choose from.
- Give people who are willing to help others with something to do.
- While you may want to communicate the importance of the issue, be careful not to normalize suicide.
- Emphasize that suicide can be prevented and treated successfully.
- Help distressed individuals to feel competent that they can do what needs to be done.
- Avoid giving very specific details of the tragedy.

SAY THIS	INSTEAD OF THIS
Died of suicide	Committed suicide
Suicide death	Successful attempt
Suicide attempt	Unsuccessful attempt
Person living with suicidal thoughts or behavior	Suicide ideator or attempter
Suicide	Completed suicide
(Describe the behavior)	Manipulative, cry for help, or suicidal gesture
Working with	Dealing with suicidal crisis

The Power of Words

Language matters when discussing issues of suicide; language reflects our attitudes and influences our attitudes and the attitudes of others. Words have power; words matter. The language we choose is an indicator of social injustice and has the power to shape our ideas and feelings in very insidious ways.

Phrases to Describe Suicide

For example, the phrase "committed suicide" is frowned on because it harks back to an era when suicide was considered a sin or a crime. Think about the times when we use the word "commit": "commit adultery" or "commit murder." Similarly, "successful suicide" or "unsuccessful attempt" are considered poor choices because they connote an achievement or something positive even though they result in tragic outcomes.

Putting People First

Likewise, using "suicide" as a noun to describe a person ("the suicide was wheeled into the morgue") is considered dehumanizing and reductionist. When we identify a person solely by his or her mental illness ("He is bipolar."), we have diminished that individual's wholeness. We wouldn't say, "He was a heart attack." Instead, we need to define a person by his or her life, not the manner of death, and say, "He was a person who died of suicide; he also loved to play golf, brew beer, and climb mountains." Or: "She is a teacher, writer, and animal lover who lives with a bipolar condition." So, let's put people first and focus on their resilience. Instead of "suicide attempter," we can say "they are a person who has lived through a suicide attempt."

The litmus test for talking about suicide is to substitute the word "cancer" for the word "suicide" to see if the sentence still makes sense or if it has a negative connotation. We wouldn't say "committed cancer" or "successful cancer"—we would simply say "cancer death" or "died of cancer." Thus, when it comes to suicide, we should say "suicide death" or "died of suicide."

We should also be wary of assuming intent when we use the phrases "cry for help" or "suicide gesture." This line of thinking can be a slippery slope. Instead of dismissing these suicidal behaviors as not serious, we should lean in and better understand what function they are serving in a person's life. Perhaps, we can get that need met in another way.

"Suicide Is Selfish"

In his book *Myths about Suicide,* Dr. Thomas Joiner goes to great lengths to dispute this common narrative of suicide as a selfish act. While it may appear that those who die of suicide are not taking into consideration the impact that their death will have on loved ones, there is much evidence to the contrary. The mind of a suicidal person is distorted and often holds the belief that he or she will be lessening their burden on loved ones by no longer being around. Avoid using this type of storyline.

"It Was His Choice"

The idea of choice or free will is often discouraged when talking about suicide because thinking is often very impaired at the time of death. Sometimes individuals who are in the throes of unimaginable emotional pain are not entirely competent to make a rational decision because their depression, addiction, or other mental health condition often prevents them from generating alternative solutions to their problems? Many people I have interviewed who have survived a very intense suicide crisis report that they have experienced something akin to command hallucinations right before they attempted—voices inside their heads telling them to kill themselves.

At an American Association of Suicidology conference, Donna Schuurman challenged the audience to look up definitions of suicide. So I did. *Merriam-Webster*[2] defines it as "the act or an instance of taking one's own life voluntarily and intentionally."

The concept of "choice" is confusing because, while we never have direct access to the inner workings of a mind of someone who has died by suicide, there is much evidence that the thought processes are often gravely disordered by the effects of trauma, mental health conditions, and substance abuse. If a person can't choose rationally due to impairment of the mind, the decision is not a choice.

The concept of "choice" is especially confusing to those bereaved by suicide. On the one hand, survivors of suicide loss who tried to keep their loved ones alive over time find the notion comforting; even though they did all they could to prolong life, the final "decision" ultimately rested with the suicidal individual. On the other hand, survivors of suicide loss sometimes cannot fathom why their loved ones would choose death over love or the possibility of a better life.

Getting Positive Messages Out There: Hope, Strength, and Healing

A few passionate resilience advocates can only go so far in changing the culture of mental health promotion and suicide prevention; we need workplaces, schools, faith communities, and healthcare systems to help model safe and compassionate language to help challenge the misinformation and myths that exist. We must learn to effectively disseminate our messages to large numbers of people. To do this, we need to craft safe and powerful messages, work collaboratively with traditional media outlets, and strategically use social media.

Crafting Effective Messages About Suicide: Hope Is the Antidote

Suicide prevention is a hard sell. As a result, well-meaning health professionals often make serious errors when crafting messages for suicide prevention. We have a tendency to think that we need to grab the public's attention through graphic and scary messages when that just tends to turn people off. Instead, we need to think about aligning with our audience's beliefs, values, priorities, and needs.[3] We must craft messages that are positively engaging, provide people with the information we want them to remember, and give them action steps.

Instead of just "raising awareness" by sharing statistics of suicide death, we can inspire hope by sharing stories of recovery and letting them know that help is available. Kevin Hines's story is one that has been spreading a ripple of hope around the world. Mr. Hines survived a jump off the Golden Gate Bridge, and his BuzzFeed video now has over 100,000 views. His main message—you are not alone, and brain health is possible. He is a fierce advocate for mental wellness and lives his message of fighting for a passion for life every day.

Another positive media campaign, developed by the National Suicide Prevention Lifeline encourages everyone to #BeThe1To to take action to prevent suicide. The campaign is designed to be adapted to many different communities to help them move from awareness to proactive prevention—because no one should die in isolation and despair.

So in conclusion, we must talk about suicide if we are going to get in front of it. But HOW we talk about suicide matters. Unsafe messages and data that leaves us feeling that "suicide is an epidemic" can create harm. Instead, let's focus on messages and stories that inspire hope and healing, and share resources that help people through their despair.

Notes

1. Suicide Prevention Resource Center, "At-a-Glance: Safe Reporting on Suicide," 2007, accessed on August 1, 2010, from http://www.sprc.org/library/at_a_glance .pdf.

2. Retrieved on November 21, 2017, from https://www.merriam-webster.com /dictionary/suicide.

3. A. Dealy, "Using Evaluation Data To Motivate and Persuade," presentation at the Garrett Lee Smith Campus Grantee Meeting, Orlando, Florida, February 4, 2010.

Chapter 3

Are Barriers to Treatment a Problem in the United States?

Insurance Coverage Reveals Mental Health Care's Pros and Cons

LARKR

LARKR is a startup that provides accessible mental health care through its mobile platform and provider network.

Most individual and small group health insurance plans are required to cover mental health and substance abuse services. However, using health insurance can be interpreted quite differently when dealing with care for the body versus care for the mind. There are many little-known factors to consider that should be carefully looked into when deciding the best options to pay for your mental health care.

To help you decide whether or not to use insurance for your mental health care, here are a few factors to consider:

Reduced Costs for Prescribed Medications

For those who are diagnosed with a mental illness and are prescribed medications, oftentimes medical insurance can significantly lower the out-of-pocket costs that you have to pay. For those who have illnesses that rely on medicated treatment, but don't have the funds to frequently purchase prescriptions on their own, this aspect of medical insurance is extremely beneficial.

It is important to note, however, that even if you are seeing a therapist for talk therapy and paying out of pocket, many insurance carriers will still cover your prescribed medications from a psychiatrist. With LARKR, the mobile platform is largely focused on talk therapy and psychiatric drug prescriptions are widely available through medical doctors. In some cases, those costs may even be eliminated.

"The Pros and Cons of Using Health Insurance for Mental Health Care," LARKR, February 12, 2018. Reprinted by permission.

Pre-Existing Conditions Don't Impact Coverage

Currently under the Affordable Care Act, all Marketplace plans must cover behavioral health treatment (i.e. psychotherapy and counseling), mental and behavioral health services, and substance abuse disorders. In addition, Marketplace plans cannot legally deny coverage and/or charge more for pre-existing medically diagnosed mental health conditions. Therefore, regardless of the reason you are seeking mental health care, Marketplace plans are required to have a package that can provide services for your needs.

There are two things to watch out for though: changes in legislation and caps on number of visits. There have already been proposals to eliminate or limit the pre-existing condition clause in recent legislation. Healthcare is a constantly changing field so it's important to know that these changes to pre-existing conditions are relatively new and many experts don't consider them to be permanent changes in our healthcare system. Additionally, many insurance plans limit the number of times you can see a therapist. While some plans may allow you to see someone for a year without interruption, other plans may only allow for 10 sessions while others require you and/or your therapist to file for allowances to extend the number of sessions allowed.

Difficulty Finding a Therapist Who Accepts Insurance

Until trying to utilize insurance, most people don't realize that the majority of mental health professionals do not take insurance. It can be frustrating trying to find a therapist who takes your insurance and when you finally do, often times people aren't happy with their limited choices.

A major reason why many therapists chose not to take insurance is reflective of the poor relationship between therapists and insurance companies. Usually, working with insurance can cause therapists to make significantly less money or take on an enormous amount of paperwork for which they are not compensated. Therapists require a master's degree and years of registered intern hours before obtaining their license. Yet after their expenses, it's possible for many to work more than 50 hours a week making less than $50,000 a year.

As a result, therapists who agree to work with insurance companies come few and far between, thus causing extensive wait times for clients. Going through your insurance company to see a therapist can have a wait time of up to four months before having your first session. Those kinds of extended wait times are just not practical when dealing with a mental issue.

Required Mental Illness Diagnosis

One of the main reasons that therapists and mental health clinics decline the use of insurance is that insurance companies typically only cover services that are declared as a medical necessity. In other words, your clinician is required to diagnose you with a mental illness in order for the services to qualify for coverage under insurance.

With the ups and downs in life that many people go through every day, many people seek mental health treatment for reasons that are not defined by a specific mental health disorder. If the reason that you are seeking a therapist is not a diagnosable disorder, like OCD or BiPolar Disorder, then it can be quite difficult to get your insurance to cover the sessions.

Being that many people go to therapy to repair relationships, recover from a traumatic experience or just generally to improve their lives, finding a medical diagnosis is often not applicable. As frustrating as this can be for patients, it would be unethical for a therapist to diagnose someone with a mental illness that they don't really have, just for the sake of using insurance and doing so can result in the therapist losing their license.

Documented Sessions and Lack of Confidentiality

Another reason that therapists are hesitant to accept insurance from their patients is due to the fact that any documented health treatment filed through your insurance is required to be recorded on your permanent medical record.

In addition to your treatment being permanently filed, health insurance companies have access to the type of treatment that you receive and what your progress has been. Any details and private information that your therapist has, your insurance company would have. If an insurance company decides to do an audit on your records in an attempt to prevent fraud, they would have access to details about what happened during each of your therapy sessions and other private details that patients would normally prefer to be left confidential. Using health insurance to receive mental health care opens a floodgate of your personal information to anyone who has access to your account at your insurance company.

Also, when such a mental health diagnosis is filed on your record, it is considered a pre-existing condition. In the future, this could potentially increase the costs of your insurance or prevent you from getting coverage altogether. When thinking about your mental health care in the long-term, this is a major factor that should be taken into consideration.

Lack of Specialists

Even if you find a therapist through your insurance, it often won't be someone who specializes in your area of need.

When a clinician signs a contract with an insurance company, they are required to provide services for any and all patients that request to book a session. This means that if you would like to see a therapist for anxiety, you may instead be stuck with a therapist who specializes in couples and families, simply because that's what your insurance company has to offer.

Contrary to popular belief, many therapists want to take insurance. Clinicians get into the profession of therapy with the main goal to help people improve people's lives. But the reduced rates, extensive paperwork and rigid restrictions that are imposed on therapists by the insurance companies has pushed many of the most talented therapists away from working on insurance panels.

Insurance benefits should be weighed and researched carefully when considering their use for mental health care. We know that life can be complicated enough and figuring out the best way to access your mental health care shouldn't add to it. That's why LARKR provides easy, affordable and private mental health treatment that is accessible on-the-go for the millions of people in need every day.

Rural Patients Struggle to Find Local Mental Health Care Providers

Kevin R. Tarlow, Carly E. McCord, Timothy R. Elliott, and Daniel F. Brossart

Kevin R. Tarlow is an assistant professor in the department of psychology at Hampton University in Virginia Carly E. McCord is a clinical research assistant professor in Texas A&M University's department of psychiatry and is also director of telebehavioral health in the university's College of Medicine. Timothy R. Elliott is an educational psychology professor in Texas A&M University's College of Education and Human Development. Daniel F. Brossart is an associate professor in the counseling psychology program in Texas A&M University's department of educational psychology.

Over 3.8 million of the 60 million rural United States residents live in Texas, which has more rural residents than any state in the country. Approximately one in four rural residents has a mental illness or substance abuse problem. However, the resources available to individuals living in rural areas are not equivalent to those available to their urban counterparts due to barriers such as lack of transportation, geographic isolation, low socioeconomic status, low educational attainment, and low rates of insurance coverage. For instance, even though some mental health diagnoses occur at least as often in rural areas as in urban ones, the negative impact of those diagnoses on health and quality of life may be greater in rural areas because of the barriers to availability, accessibility, and perceived stigma of mental health care services. Rural-urban health disparities have been reported in groups ranging from clergy to veterans.

"Health-Related Quality of Life of Rural Clients Seeking Telepsychology Services," by Kevin R. Tarlow, Carly E. McCord, Timothy R. Elliott and Daniel F. Brossart, *International Journal of Telemedicine and Applications*, November 19, 2014. https://www.hindawi.com /journals/ijta/2014/168158/. Licensed under CC BY 3.0.

Not only are rural residents confronted with unique barriers to service, but health care providers are less likely to deliver services in rural areas due to lower wages and compensation, increased ethical risk, and higher burn-out rates. Given the range of rural health needs and the scarcity of specialty services, providers who do offer services in rural communities are often pressured to treat patients at the limits of their knowledge and expertise. The unique features of the rural health care landscape require health policies, legislation, and interventions informed by these issues.

Telehealth, or the use of telecommunication technologies to provide health care services at a distance, is one way to offset the disparities in health care access found in rural areas. Telehealth describes a broad range of health-related services that may include use of internet, telephone, videoconferencing, email, chat, text messaging, and other technologies to improve access, affordability, and efficiency of service delivery. The American Psychological Association (APA) recently recognized the benefits of using telepsychology (i.e., psychological telehealth services) to increase access to underserved areas. For the purposes of this paper, the term telepsychology is used to describe the delivery of individual psychotherapy via secure videoconferencing technology. In their guidelines for the use of this emerging treatment modality, APA suggested that health service providers should utilize telepsychology when research evidence supports its use for a particular client or population (p. 8). However, APA also pointed out that outcomes research for telepsychology may be lacking for many clients due to the developing nature of the field. The purpose of this paper is to (a) better understand the health needs of rural clients seeking mental health care services and (b) establish an evidence basis for telepsychology's effectiveness with rural clients. Meeting these two goals is an important step to increasing mental health care access for underserved rural areas.

A major challenge to providing health care services to rural communities—telehealth or otherwise—is the diversity of the rural communities themselves. As sociologist Daryl Hobbs said,

"When you have seen *one* rural community, you have seen *one* rural community" (emphasis in original, p. 397). Rural health policies and interventions should be empirically and *locally* informed, based on the needs and resources of each unique community. Creating sustainable initiatives to meet health needs in rural areas often requires local collaboration among community stakeholders, including clinicians, researchers, students, community leaders, and other policy makers.

Understanding a rural community's available health resources is a vital first step in locally informed policy and intervention development. Community capacity describes a community's ability to mobilize its social, political, and organizational capital to meet unmet needs. This begins with an assessment of needs and is followed by the development of deliberate, collaborative intervention strategies. The "build it and they will come" mentality will not lead to sustainability in rural areas. Universities may be powerful facilitators of community capacity, but they must collaborate with local stakeholders and maintain those relationships beyond their inception.

In 2006, the Center for Community Health Development (CCHD) at the Texas A&M Health Science Center (http://www.cchd.us/) conducted a survey in the Brazos Valley—a region of Texas comprised of seven counties, all of which are federally designated Health Professional Shortage Areas (HPSAs). Texas has the highest percentage of HPSAs in the country. The 2006 survey found that mental health and public transportation were among the top needs of the region. Over half of respondents reported having at least one day of "poor mental health" in the last month, and 62% of respondents reported needing mental health services and being unable to get the needed services.

In response to the identified health needs of the area, a "town and gown" partnership was created between Leon County (one of the seven Brazos Valley counties) and Texas A&M University to provide telepsychology services to the area. A locally appointed health resource commission mobilized resources in Leon County to provide a physical location to conduct the telepsychology services, and in 2009 advanced doctoral level students in the Counseling Psychology program at Texas A&M University began providing long-distance services under the supervision of a licensed psychologist.

It was expected that many Leon County residents seeking telepsychology services would present with cooccurring physical and mental health conditions. Consequently, assessment of client needs, issues, and response to telepsychology treatment required an evaluation of client health-related quality of life (HRQOL). HRQOL is a multidimensional construct of well-being often encompassing physical, mental, emotional, and social functioning. The Centers for Disease Control and Prevention (CDC) suggest that measures such as the Medical Outcomes Study Short Form (SF-12) can be used to identify needed services, inform policy and legislation, and evaluate outcomes of health interventions.

Three other studies of similar size have evaluated the impact of telepsychology and telemedicine for mental health treatment on HRQOL using the SF-12v2. In one Canadian study, telepsychiatry outperformed in-person psychiatry for mental health improvement. In two European studies that included German-speaking clients in The Netherlands, Germany, Austria, and Switzerland, internet-based cognitive behavioral therapy (CBT) interventions for grief and post-traumatic stress disorder (PTSD) outperformed the waitlist control group for mental health improvement. While all three studies found moderate to large effects of telehealth interventions on mental health status, no effects on physical health status were detected.

The current study was developed with two goals. First, given the barriers to health experienced by many rural communities, we wish to better understand the physical and mental health status of rural residents receiving telepsychology services. We compare the physical and mental health scores for participants in the current study with established HRQOL norms for the overall US population and with a national sample of depressed individuals.

We expect that participants presenting for telepsychology services will have a lower HRQOL than both the national standardization sample and the national sample of depressed individuals. We also briefly review the depressive symptoms reported by participants in order to better describe the clinical features of the sample.

Second, we examine the possible impact of telepsychology services on client HRQOL in this underserved area. We expect that participants who received four sessions of telepsychology services will demonstrate significant improvements in mental health status. However, we were uncertain of the degree to which telepsychology services would affect physical health functioning.

These two goals are independent but related: What are the physical and mental health needs of this population? And given barriers to other health services, is telepsychology an effective treatment option for this group? Answering these questions is essential for empirically and locally informed health policy development. We expect that a range of stakeholders in and outside of the Brazos Valley would benefit from a better understanding of (a) the HRQOL of this rural community and (b) the increased health service options made possible by emerging areas such as telepsychology.

[...]

Discussion

This study found that the health-related quality of life (HRQOL) of rural Texas residents presenting for telepsychology services is indeed poor. While participants in this study reported physical health problems, their mental health status was exceptionally low, with the average participant's mental health status score falling about two standard deviations below the average for the US population. Individuals seeking telepsychology services had even lower mental health scores than a national sample of individuals diagnosed with major depressive disorder. This finding is consistent with other studies of rural and urban HRQOL differences.

Providing psychological services to clients in a Health Professional Shortage Area (HPSA) poses several challenges. Individuals seeking treatment are expected to present with cooccurring physical and mental health diagnoses, as was the case in the current study's sample. Many clients in this study's sample reported a range of chronic health and disability issues in addition to psychological concerns such as depression, trauma, substance abuse, and anxiety. Even with access to telepsychology services, many clients (and their counselors) may be undertreated for their physical health concerns. The ongoing lack of care experienced in rural HPSAs has clear implications for the provision of telepsychology services.

Despite the complexity of their presenting physical and mental health concerns, we found that telepsychology was effective at improving the mental health status of clients who were assessed after four sessions of therapy. These results add to the growing evidence base for telepsychology, and they show that this emerging treatment modality may be effective specifically for rural residents living in an underserved area. Our findings may be of special importance to health care providers in rural areas who have been encouraged to utilize telepsychology when outcomes research supports its use for that particular population.

While working in rural areas has its challenges, it is not without opportunities. As was seen in this study, utilizing academic-community partnerships provides opportunities to train future professionals in innovative service delivery models. There is also the potential for more collaborative care for health care consumers. In urban areas, it is virtually impossible for all the health providers to be familiar with the dozens or even hundreds of other providers in the area. But due to the small number of providers in rural areas, providers have the ability to know the names and faces of all other providers in the community. If interorganizational communication is encouraged and expected, community capacity can be built and consumers can expect more integrated care.

Sixty-two percent of individuals surveyed in the rural Brazos Valley region of Texas report being unable to access needed mental health services. Given the numerous barriers to health experienced by many rural communities, it is possible that millions of rural US residents desire mental health care but are unable to access it. This study demonstrates that telepsychology services developed through an academic-community partnership are a viable option for rural residents in need of effective mental health care. Telepsychology is an emerging area of telehealth and telemedicine with rapidly growing evidence for its effectiveness, and its high accessibility has special implications for rural communities.

Limitations of the current study include the relatively small sample size, although this is a necessary aspect of studying groups living in sparsely populated areas. Due to the small number of participants, subsequent analyses lacked the statistical power to measure possible effects of gender or race/ethnicity on treatment outcome. While the focus of this study was on the response to a brief treatment (four sessions), future studies should also investigate the impact of long-term treatment, especially given the chronic nature of many rural clients' presenting concerns. Counselors in the current study did not conduct a comprehensive assessment of all physical and mental health needs of clients; while global measures of HRQOL were used for this analysis, future studies may wish to investigate the prevalence and impact of specific diagnoses on response to telepsychology treatment. No clients were excluded from the study as long as they did not meet clinical exclusion criteria (e.g., high suicidal or homicidal risk, active psychosis); however several individuals seeking telepsychology treatment were unable to receive services because of mobility restrictions. All sessions were conducted at the community health center in Leon County, and individuals without cars were unable to attend weekly sessions. While this is a limitation of this study's design, many telehealth and telemedicine interventions use technology to deliver services directly to patients' homes. Telepsychology researchers may wish to study in-home services as well; however special considerations should be made to ensure client confidentiality and safety.

The Mentally Ill Self-Medicate Because They're Not Getting Proper Care

American Addiction Centers

American Addiction Centers (AAC) provides customized treatment to adults with both substance abuse problems and mental health disorders. AAC is based in Brentwood, Tennessee.

The National Institute of Mental Health (NIMH) reports that in 2015 nearly 18 percent of adults in the United States suffered from some form of mental illness, often termed any mental illness, or AMI. Almost 10 million American adults, which is 4 percent of the population, battled serious mental illness (SMI) in 2015, NIMH further publishes.

Often, medications are part of treatment for mental illness to stabilize brain chemistry and improve life functioning. Individuals struggling with mental illness may attempt to medicate symptoms on their own by taking mind-altering drugs or drinking alcohol. Drugs and alcohol can also interact with brain chemistry, serving to enhance pleasure and reduce stress and anxiety.

For someone suffering from mental illness, drugs and alcohol may seem to help them "balance" difficult symptoms related to the disorder. This practice is called self-medicating, and while it may seem to work in the short-term, self-medication can lead to many risks and can even make mental illness worse in the long run.

Common Drugs Used for Self-Medication of Mental Illness

Substance abuse is extremely common among people who struggle with mental illness, as the US Department of Health and Human Services (HHS) reports that as many as one out every four Americans who battle serious mental health concerns also has

"The Concerns of Self-Medicating Mental Illness," American Addiction Centers, September 27, 2017. Reprinted by permission.

issues with substance abuse. People struggling with depression, anxiety disorders, personality disorders, and schizophrenia are the most likely to also have issues with substance abuse.

Depression can induce overwhelming sadness, sleep issues, and trouble coping, which may be temporarily alleviated with drugs and/or alcohol. People who struggle with bipolar disorder, a mood disorder that involves significant mood swings from mania to depression, abuse alcohol and drugs at very high rates as well. *Psychiatric Times* reports that around half of those battling bipolar disorder will struggle with issues involving alcohol abuse.

Anxiety disorders, like social anxiety disorder, may make it hard for people to function normally in everyday life, and drugs and alcohol can temporarily blunt anxiety and make social interaction easier as they lower inhibitions. Alcohol and drugs may also commonly be used to self-medicate the difficult recurring symptoms of post-traumatic stress disorder, another anxiety disorder.

Symptoms of personality disorders, such as borderline personality disorder (BPD), can make it difficult for a person to carry out everyday tasks, making drugs seem like a happy diversion. Schizophrenia is a serious mental illness, and individuals suffering from the disorder regularly turn to drugs and alcohol as a method of tempering psychotic symptoms.

Below are some of the most commonly used drugs for self-medicating symptoms of mental illness and why:

- *Alcohol*: Interacting with brain chemistry to lower anxiety, increase happiness, decrease inhibitions, and heighten sociability, alcohol is a common substance used to alleviate stress and symptoms of mental illness. Alcohol is a depressant, and it slows functions of the central nervous system, helping to promote relaxation and calmness. Alcohol can therefore temporarily relieve tension and enhance mellow feelings.
- *Stimulants like cocaine and methamphetamine*: Stimulant drugs greatly enhance pleasure by causing a spike of dopamine in the brain. Dopamine is one of the brain's

neurotransmitters that sends signals telling a person to be happy. Stimulants can also increase energy, focus, and attention, and help a person to stay awake for long periods of time while suppressing appetite.

- *Opioids like heroin and prescription painkillers:* These substances elevate happiness and mellow feelings while also acting as central nervous system depressants and blunting anxiety and stress, reducing tension, and increasing relaxation and sedation.
- *Marijuana:* Commonly used to help people "chill," marijuana has both hallucinogenic and depressant effects, altering perceptions and enhancing relaxation. Marijuana may alter moods and help people to sleep.
- *Depressant drugs, including tranquilizers and sedatives:* Often prescribed to treat mental illness, these prescription drugs can also be abused when used without a legitimate prescription. They help to reduce anxiety and depressed moods while enhancing sleep functions and stabilizing brain chemistry.

Risks of Mixing Drugs with Mental Illness

Medications are often highly beneficial in treating symptoms of mental illness, but only when used as directed under the supervision of a medical or mental health provider. Prescription medications are often an important aspect of a complete treatment plan. When mental illness goes undiagnosed, or symptoms are not being properly managed, it may encourage a person to attempt to medicate these troubling symptoms on their own, however. Self-medication can be highly dangerous.

Drugs and alcohol can have unpredictable side effects and can interfere with any medications a person may already be taking, making them less effective or even having more serious consequences, such as a potential toxic reaction leading to a life-threatening overdose. Drug and alcohol abuse can also increase the intensity and possible side effects associated with the mental illness, leading to more issues and possible problems. Mood swings can be more significant, and psychotic symptoms may be more likely as well when abusing substances.

While under the influence of drugs or alcohol, a person may take bigger risks and get involved in situations that can be potentially hazardous, which can also be compounded by the fact that many mental illnesses also include impulsivity and a lack of regard for consequences as side effects. Accidents, injuries, unwanted pregnancy, criminal behaviors, and increased odds for contracting a sexually transmitted or infectious disease are all possible consequences of self-medicating mental illness.

The "crash" that can follow the "high" produced by substance abuse can also be compounded when a mental illness is also present. Depression and anxiety can then worsen. The Office of National Drug Control Policy publishes that teenagers who are depressed are twice as likely to abuse illicit drugs, including marijuana, than adolescents who are not depressed. Marijuana use can greatly increase suicidal thoughts as well as raise the odds for engaging in other risky behaviors like additional drug abuse, heavy alcohol consumption, or daily cigarette smoking.

Withdrawal side effects of alcohol and drugs can make a person more likely to continue abusing substances to avoid these negative side effects, which are only exacerbated if a person also battles mental illness, *Psych Central* warns. Substance abuse in the presence of a mental illness increases the risk for developing drug dependence and suffering from addiction. The journal *Addiction Science & Clinical Practice* reports that mental illness and addiction are complexly intertwined; each condition makes the other worse and may lead to the onset of one or the other.

Treatments for Co-Occurring Disorders

According to the 2014 National Survey on Drug Use and Health (NSDUH), over 21 million American adults struggled with addiction involving drugs and/or alcohol. Nearly 8 million adults in the United States battled both addiction and mental illness at the same time in 2014, the Substance Abuse and Mental Health

Services Administration (SAMHSA) reports. When both mental illness and addiction are diagnosed in the same person at the same time, the disorders are said to be *co-occurring*, and specialized treatment is optimal for recovery.

Half of those who battle SMI and one-third of the individuals struggling with AMI also abuse substances, the National Alliance on Mental Illness (NAMI) publishes. Substance abuse may provide a temporary balance, or reprieve, to mental illness symptoms; however, in reality, self-medication only serves to make things worse. Brain chemistry is altered by drugs and alcohol, and similar brain regions may also be related to the onset of mental illness. Substance abuse only increases the potential imbalance, making symptoms worse, and making it difficult for treatment methods to work as intended. Depression, anxiety, sleep issues, appetite alterations, irritability, restlessness, trouble thinking clearly, suicidal ideations, psychosis, and mood swings are common side effects of addiction, all of which may also be symptoms of mental illness.

Drug dependence is a side effect of addiction, and withdrawal symptoms that occur after drugs process out of the body can be significant. These withdrawal symptoms are even more intense and pronounced when a co-occurring mental illness is also present. Withdrawal can be particularly intense then for someone battling mental illness, and professional help is often needed to help the drugs safely process out of the body.

A medical detox program can help to manage cravings and withdrawal symptoms while minimizing relapse. Medications are often an important aspect of medical detox, and in the case of co-occurring disorders, all medical and mental health providers need to work together to ensure that the necessary pharmacological tools are complementary. Medical detox is the safest way to help someone struggling with co-occurring disorders to stop taking drugs. Detox is generally the first step in a comprehensive treatment program, providing a safe and secure environment in which to achieve physical stability.

The National Institute on Drug Abuse (NIDA) publishes that a comprehensive and integrated approach is optimal to treat co-occurring disorders. This simultaneous method of treatment ensures that all members of the treatment team work together toward the same goals. Since each disorder can influence the severity and side effects of the other, they are treated at the same time. Thorough assessments and drug screenings are important before admission into a program and then throughout the treatment program to evaluate progress.

Behavioral therapies, including Cognitive Behavioral Therapy (CBT), teach healthy coping mechanisms for managing stress, anxiety, and difficult emotions. In group and individual therapy and counseling sessions, clients learn new life skills and habits for managing co-occurring disorders. Family counseling and therapy serve to educate loved ones and help in improving communication skills and the inner workings of the overall family unit. Specialized support groups also aid in providing positive social interaction, helping to dispel isolation that may be related to one or both disorders, and providing tips and tools for minimizing relapse.

Generally, residential treatment programs offer the highest standard of care, providing around-the-clock care and supervision in a structured and stable environment. Individuals may be moved between levels of care as they progress in treatment. Balanced nutrition, set sleep schedules, medication management, traditional therapeutic care, and holistic techniques can all be beneficial components of an integrated treatment program for co-occurring disorders.

Stigmatization and Barriers to Mental Health Care Are Still Problems for Black Americans

Mental Health America

Mental Health America was founded in 1909. It is a leading community-based nonprofit focused on promoting mental health among Americans and addressing the needs of those living with mental illnesses. They promote mental health through advocacy, public policy, education, research, and services.

Mental Health America works nationally and locally to raise awareness about mental health. We believe that everyone at risk for mental illnesses and related disorders should receive early and effective interventions. Historically, communities of color experience unique and considerable challenges in accessing mental health services.

Demographics/Societal Issues

- 13.2 % of the US population, or roughly 45.7 million people, identify themselves as Black or African American, according to 2014 US Census Bureau numbers. Another 2.5% identified as multiracial. This represents an increase from 12.6 percent of the US population, who identified themselves as Black/African-American in the 2010 Census.[1]
- As of 2010, 55 percent of all Black/African American people lived in the South, 18 percent lived in the Midwest, 17 percent in the Northeast, and 10 percent in the West.[2]
- Historical adversity, which includes slavery, sharecropping and race-based exclusion from health, educational, social and economic resources, translates into socioeconomic disparities experienced by African Americans today. Socioeconomic status, in turn, is linked to mental health: People who are

"Black & African American Communities and Mental Health," Mental Health America. Reprinted by permission.

impoverished, homeless, incarcerated or have substance abuse problems are at higher risk for poor mental health.

- Despite progress made over the years, racism continues to have an impact on the mental health of Black/African Americans. Negative stereotypes and attitudes of rejection have decreased, but continue to occur with measurable, adverse consequences. Historical and contemporary instances of negative treatment have led to a mistrust of authorities, many of whom are not seen as having the best interests of Black/African Americans in mind.

Prevalence

According to the US HHS Office of Minority Health[3]:

- Adult Black/African Americans are 20 percent more likely to report serious psychological distress than adult whites.
- Adult Black/African Americans living below poverty are three times more likely to report serious psychological distress than those living above poverty.
- Adult Black/African Americans are more likely to have feelings of sadness, hopelessness, and worthlessness than are adult whites.
- And while Black/African Americans are less likely than white people to die from suicide as teenagers, Black/African Americans teenagers are more likely to attempt suicide than are white teenagers (8.3 percent v. 6.2 percent).

Black/African Americans of all ages are more likely to be victims of serious violent crime than are non-Hispanic whites, making them more likely to meet the diagnostic criteria for post-traumatic stress disorder (PTSD). Black/African Americans are also twice as likely as non-Hispanic whites to be diagnosed with schizophrenia.[4]

Attitudes

According to a study conducted by Ward, Wiltshire, Detry, and Brown in 2013[5]:

- Black/African Americans hold beliefs related to stigma, psychological openness, and help-seeking, which in turn affects their coping behaviors. Generally speaking, the participants in this study were not very open to acknowledging psychological problems, but they were somewhat open to seek mental health services.
- Thirty percent of participants reported having a mental illness or receiving treatment for a mental illness.
- Black/African American men are particularly concerned about stigma.
- Cohort effects, exposure to mental illness, and increased knowledge of mental illness are factors which could potentially change beliefs about symptoms of mental illness.
- Participants appeared apprehensive about seeking professional help for mental health issues, which is consistent with previous research. However, participants were willing to seek out some form of help.

Treatment Issues

- Black/African Americans today are over-represented in our jails and prisons. People of color account for 60 percent of the prison population. Black/African Americans also account for 37 percent of drug arrests, but only 14 percent of regular drug users (illicit drug use is frequently associated with self-medication among people with mental illnesses).[6]
- Because less than 2 percent of American Psychological Association members are Black/African American, some may worry that mental health care practitioners are not culturally competent enough to treat their specific issues.[7] This is compounded by the fact that some Black/

African American patients have reported experiencing racism and microaggression from therapists.[8]

- Stigma and judgment prevents Black/African Americans from seeking treatment for their mental illnesses. Research indicates that Black/African Americans believe that mild depression or anxiety would be considered "crazy" in their social circles. Furthermore, many believe that discussions about mental illness would not be appropriate even among family.[9]

Access/Insurance

Disparities in access to care and treatment for mental illnesses have also persisted over time.

- While implementation of the Affordable Care Act has helped to close the gap in uninsured individuals, 15.9 percent of Black/African Americans, versus 11.1 percent of white Americans were still uninsured in 2014.[10]
- In 2012, the percentage of people who were unable to get or delayed in getting needed medical care, or prescription medicines was significantly higher for people with no health insurance (18.7%) than for people with private insurance (8.4%).[10]
- In 2011, 54.3 percent of adult Black/African Americans with a major depressive episode received treatment, compared with 73.1 percent of adult white Americans.[11]
- Compared to 45.3 percent of white Americans, 40.6 percent of Black/African Americans age 12 and over were treated for substance abuse and completed their treatment course, in 2010.[11]

Sources

1. United States Census Bureau. (2014). Quick facts. Retrieved from https://www.census.gov/quickfacts/table/PST120215/00

2. http://www.census.gov/newsroom/releases/archives/2010_census/cb11-cn185.html

3. US Department of Health and Human Services Office of Minority Mental Health. (2016). Mental health and African Americans. Retrieved from http://minorityhealth.hhs.gov/omh/browse.aspx?lvl=4&lvlid=24

4. American Psychological Association. (2016). African Americans have limited access to mental and behavioral health care. Retrieved from http://www.apa.org/about/gr/issues/minority/access.aspx

5. Ward, E. C., Wiltshire, J. C., Detry, M. A., & Brown, R. L. (2013). African American men and women's attitude toward mental illness, perceptions of stigma, and preferred coping behaviors. *Nursing Research, 62*(3), 185-194. doi:10.1097/NNR.0b013e31827bf533

6. http://www.americanprogress.org/issues/race/news/2012/03/13/11351/the-top-10-most-startling-facts-about-people-of-color-and-criminal-justice-in-the-united-states/, 2012

7. American Psychological Association. (2014). Demographic characteristics of APA members by membership characteristics. Retrieved from http://www.apa.org/workforce/publications/14-member/table-1.pdf

8. Williams, M. T. (2013). How therapists drive away minority clients. Psychology Today. Retrieved from https://www.psychologytoday.com/blog/culturally-speaking/201306/how-therapists-drive-away-minority-c

9. Williams, M. T. (2011). Why African Americans avoid psychotherapy. Psychology Today. Retrieved from https://www.psychologytoday.com/blog/culturally-speaking/201111/why-african-americans-avoid-psychoth

10. Agency for Healthcare Research and Quality. (2014). National healthcare quality and disparities report. Retrieved from http://www.ahrq.gov/sites/default/files/wysiwyg/research/findings/nhqrdr/2014chartbooks/access/2014n

11. Agency for Healthcare Research and Quality. (2013). National healthcare disparities report. Retrieved from http://www.ahrq.gov/research/findings/nhqrdr/nhdr13/chap2-txt.html#fig231

Teletherapy Allows Therapists to Treat Patients From Anywhere

Tori DeAngelis

Tori DeAngelis is a veteran journalist and editor whose writing focuses on psychology, health, medicine, culture, and spirituality. She is based in Syracuse, New York.

Interested in practicing virtual reality therapy? If so, it's important to get up to speed on the latest legal and ethical developments so you'll be sure to serve your clients safely, legally and effectively.

For starters, know that there is little consistent guidance across states on how psychologists should use these and other forms of electronic communication such as email, Skype and various forms of videoconferencing, says Deborah Baker, JD, director for prescriptive authority and regulatory affairs in APA's Practice Directorate. (See more on APA's work to create telehealth guidelines in the June *Monitor*.)

"While technology is pushing ahead at a rapid pace, psychology licensing laws have not yet caught up," she says. That's true in other fields as well, she notes: All health and mental health-care professions are wrestling with many of the same issues.

That said, experts in the field are beginning to develop guidelines to help psychology practitioners stay within their legal and ethical limits.

Interstate Practice

One of the biggest unresolved issues concerns telepsychology across state lines. Email, videoconferencing and avatar therapy all allow psychologists to reach patients anywhere, but state licensing laws generally do not permit out-of-state psychologists to provide telepsychology services to consumers, says Baker, who

"Practicing Distance Therapy, Legally and Ethically," by Tori DeAngelis, American Psychological Association, March 2012. Reprinted by permission.

helped conduct a 50-state review of telehealth laws in 2010. For most states, that means you may need to be licensed both in your own state and in your clients' state in order to practice with these modalities, she says.

There are exceptions, though. For example, many states have guest licensure provisions that allow out-of-state-licensed psychologists to provide services for a short period of time—ranging from 10 to 30 days in a calendar year—under specified conditions. In addition, the Association of State and Provincial Psychology Boards has created a credential called the Interjurisdictional Practice Certificate that facilitates temporary practice in other jurisdictions.

Providing distance therapy within your own state is simpler, and can help you reach people who wouldn't otherwise have access to services—rural residents or people with certain disabilities, for instance—and clients who want to receive services from home. In this case, you can confidently provide services as long as you abide by all applicable licensing requirements and professional standards of care, including understanding the technology you're using (more on that below), Baker says. A few additional steps can ensure you have the latest information in this fast-moving area, Baker adds. Make sure that you:

- Periodically check your state legislature's website for the latest state telehealth laws and regulations. If there is no telehealth law in your state, look to see if there is a board policy statement that provides guidance on telepractice, she recommends.
- Check whether your state licensing board has issued any policies related to telepsychology. As of last summer, several states, including Florida, Massachusetts, North Carolina, Texas, Virginia and Wisconsin, had such policies in place. (To contact any state board, visit the ASPPB website.)
- Contact your malpractice insurance carrier to confirm that telehealth services—both in-state and across jurisdictional lines—are covered under your malpractice policy. They are

likely to be covered for in-state practice but not necessarily for interjurisdictional practice, Baker says.

Three states—California, Vermont and Kentucky—have already passed laws specifying psychologists' legal obligations in online therapy. For instance, Kentucky states that at the outset, a psychologist using telehealth must obtain the patient's informed consent, which includes documenting whether the patient has the necessary knowledge and skills to benefit from telehealth. Similarly, California requires that providers obtain both written and verbal informed consent before providing telehealth services, including a description of the potential risks, consequences, and benefits of telemedicine. The state does not, however, appear to extend this requirement to consultations between providers where the patient is not directly involved, Baker says.

Ethical Telepractice

The ethics of telepsychology are in a similar state of flux, though there is a lot of good information available, says Jeffrey Barnett, PsyD, professor of psychology at Loyola University Maryland, who regularly teaches and writes about ethical issues in psychology. Included are telepsychology guidelines developed by both the Canadian Psychological Association and the Ohio Psychological Association.

In general, all of the standards of the APA ethics code apply, says Barnett. That includes standards on informed consent, competence to practice, confidentiality, doing no harm, and on how terminations, interruption of service and payment arrangements are handled.

"In fact, practicing with distance therapies actually raises the bar, because you also need to be competent in the media you're using," he says. To this end, get training in using the hardware and software involved in the treatment you plan to provide, Barnett recommends. For example, to preserve confidentiality and therefore meet the requirements of the Health Insurance Portability and Accountability Act, learn how to use encryption software, and for maximum ease of communication between you and your client, how to set up your equipment to provide good sound and visual resolution. You also need training on how to deal with some of the limits of telepsychology. With avatar therapy, for instance, you can't read a patient's expressions or body language, though some of that is changing due to advances in technology.

Fortunately, there are many continuing education workshops on these topics, says Barnett. If you're unsure how to proceed, contact your state, provincial or territorial psychological association's ethics committee, the APA Ethics Office, your state licensing board, or knowledgeable colleagues, he recommends.

In addition, when using these technologies, it's important to conduct an initial assessment of each client to determine his or her appropriateness for telepsychology, says Barnett. A client who is suicidal, for example, may require much more active and intensive services than telepsychology can provide. Other factors to consider include making sure you have provided adequate emergency contact information in case your distance client faces a crisis, and ensuring that your patient's privacy and confidentiality are adequately protected by encrypting electronic transmissions and records, he says.

Barnett has an article covering these and more topics in the June 2011 issue *Psychotherapy*.

A new APA Task Force on the Development of Telepsychology Guidelines for Psychologists should further clarify psychologists' rights and obligations soon. The 10-member group—which includes representatives from APA, ASPPB and the APA Insurance Trust—met in July to review the area and discuss results of a survey sent to all APA governance groups, state associations, state and provincial psychology boards, telepractice-related organizations and interested individuals.

The group has developed a working plan and will begin drafting guidelines in the next several months. In addition, the task force is creating a Web page that will provide information about the task force's work and calls for comments, and will publicize this information in other APA venues as well.

Putting the proper safeguards in place should help to ensure that telehealth technologies live up to their promise of improving care, Barnett adds.

"There are a lot of good data showing that you can form a good therapeutic alliance using telepsychology, and that these modalities can help people with all sorts of issues," Barnett says. "Now we just need to develop the formal guidelines, and hopefully the laws and regulations, to make this a successful and safe area of practice."

Mental Health Patients Have More Treatment Options Than Ever

OpenStax College

Launched in 2012 by Rice University, OpenStax College is an academic nonprofit that produces peer-reviewed textbooks, which the public can access for free in digital form or for a low cost in print form.

Before we explore the various approaches to therapy used today, let's begin our study of therapy by looking at how many people experience mental illness and how many receive treatment. According to the US Department of Health and Human Services (2013), 19% of US adults experienced mental illness in 2012. For teens (ages 13–18), the rate is similar to that of adults, and for children ages 8–15, current estimates suggest that 13% experience mental illness in a given year.

With many different treatment options available, approximately how many people receive mental health treatment per year? According to the Substance Abuse and Mental Health Services Administration (SAMHSA), in 2008, 13.4% of adults received treatment for a mental health issue. These percentages reflect the number of adults who received care in inpatient and outpatient settings and/or used prescription medication for psychological disorders.

Children and adolescents also receive mental health services. The Centers for Disease Control and Prevention's National Health and Nutrition Examination Survey (NHANES) found that approximately half (50.6%) of children with mental disorders had received treatment for their disorder within the past year. However, there were some differences between treatment rates by category of disorder. For example, children with anxiety disorders were least likely to have received treatment in the past year, while children with ADHD or a conduct disorder were more likely to receive treatment. Can you think of some possible reasons for these differences in receiving treatment?

Considering the many forms of treatment for mental health disorders available today, how did these forms of treatment emerge? Let's take a look at the history of mental health treatment from the past (with some questionable approaches in light of modern understanding of mental illness) to where we are today.

Treatment in the Past

For much of history, the mentally ill have been treated very poorly. It was believed that mental illness was caused by demonic possession, witchcraft, or an angry god. For example, in medieval times, abnormal behaviors were viewed as a sign that a person was possessed by demons. If someone was considered to be possessed, there were several forms of treatment to release spirits from the individual. The most common treatment was exorcism, often conducted by priests or other religious figures: Incantations and prayers were said over the person's body, and she may have been given some medicinal drinks. Another form of treatment for extreme cases of mental illness was trephining: A small hole was made in the afflicted individual's skull to release spirits from the body. Most people treated in this manner died. In addition to exorcism and trephining, other practices involved execution or imprisonment of people with psychological disorders. Still others were left to be homeless beggars. Generally speaking, most people who exhibited strange behaviors were greatly misunderstood and treated cruelly. The prevailing theory of psychopathology in earlier history was the idea that mental illness was the result of demonic possession by either an evil spirit or an evil god because early beliefs incorrectly attributed all unexplainable phenomena to deities deemed either good or evil.

From the late 1400s to the late 1600s, a common belief perpetuated by some religious organizations was that some people made pacts with the devil and committed horrible acts, such as eating babies. These people were considered to be witches and were tried and condemned by courts—they were often burned at the stake. Worldwide, it is estimated that tens of thousands of mentally ill people were killed after being accused of being witches or under the influence of witchcraft.

By the 18th century, people who were considered odd and unusual were placed in asylums. Asylums were the first institutions created for the specific purpose of housing people with psychological disorders, but the focus was ostracizing them from society rather than treating their disorders. Often these people were kept in windowless dungeons, beaten, chained to their beds, and had little to no contact with caregivers.

In the late 1700s, a French physician, Philippe Pinel, argued for more humane treatment of the mentally ill. He suggested that they be unchained and talked to, and that's just what he did for patients at La Salpêtrière in Paris in 1795. Patients benefited from this more humane treatment, and many were able to leave the hospital.

In the 19th century, Dorothea Dix led reform efforts for mental health care in the United States. She investigated how those who are mentally ill and poor were cared for, and she discovered an underfunded and unregulated system that perpetuated abuse of this population. Horrified by her findings, Dix began lobbying various state legislatures and the US Congress for change. Her efforts led to the creation of the first mental asylums in the United States.

Despite reformers' efforts, however, a typical asylum was filthy, offered very little treatment, and often kept people for decades. At Willard Psychiatric Center in upstate New York, for example, one treatment was to submerge patients in cold baths for long periods of time. Electroshock treatment was also used, and the way the treatment was administered often broke patients' backs; in 1943, doctors at Willard administered 1,443 shock treatments. (Electroshock is now called electroconvulsive treatment, and the therapy is still used, but with safeguards and under anesthesia. A brief application of electric stimulus is used to produce a generalized seizure. Controversy continues over its effectiveness versus the side effects.) Many of the wards and rooms were so cold that a glass of water would be frozen by morning. Willard's doors were not closed until 1995. Conditions like these remained commonplace until well into the 20th century.

Starting in 1954 and gaining popularity in the 1960s, antipsychotic medications were introduced. These proved a tremendous help in controlling the symptoms of certain psychological disorders, such as psychosis. Psychosis was a common diagnosis of individuals in mental hospitals, and it was often evidenced by symptoms like hallucinations and delusions, indicating a loss of contact with reality. Then in 1963, Congress passed and John F. Kennedy signed the Mental Retardation Facilities and Community Mental Health Centers Construction Act, which provided federal support and funding for community mental health centers. This legislation changed how mental health services were delivered in the United States. It started the process of deinstitutionalization, the closing of large asylums, by providing for people to stay in their communities and be treated locally. In 1955, there were 558,239 severely mentally ill patients institutionalized at public hospitals. By 1994, by percentage of the population, there were 92% fewer hospitalized individuals.

Mental Health Treatment Today

Today, there are community mental health centers across the nation. They are located in neighborhoods near the homes of clients, and they provide large numbers of people with mental health services of various kinds and for many kinds of problems. Unfortunately, part of what occurred with deinstitutionalization was that those released from institutions were supposed to go to newly created centers, but the system was not set up effectively. Centers were underfunded, staff was not trained to handle severe illnesses such as schizophrenia, there was high staff burnout, and no provision was made for the other services people needed, such as housing, food, and job training. Without these supports, those people released under deinstitutionalization often ended up homeless. Even today, a large portion of the homeless population is considered to be mentally ill. Statistics show that 26% of homeless adults living in shelters experience mental illness.

Another group of the mentally ill population is involved in the corrections system. According to a 2006 special report by the Bureau of Justice Statistics (BJS), approximately 705,600 mentally ill adults were incarcerated in the state prison system, and another 78,800 were incarcerated in the federal prison system. A further 479,000 were in local jails. According to the study, "people with mental illnesses are overrepresented in probation and parole populations at estimated rates ranging from two to four times the general population." The Treatment Advocacy Center reported that the growing number of mentally ill inmates has placed a burden on the correctional system.

Today, instead of asylums, there are psychiatric hospitals run by state governments and local community hospitals focused on short-term care. In all types of hospitals, the emphasis is on short-term stays, with the average length of stay being less than two weeks and often only several days. This is partly due to the very high cost of psychiatric hospitalization, which can be about $800 to $1000 per night. Therefore, insurance coverage often limits the length of time a person can be hospitalized for treatment. Usually individuals are hospitalized only if they are an imminent threat to themselves or others.

Most people suffering from mental illnesses are not hospitalized. If someone is feeling very depressed, complains of hearing voices, or feels anxious all the time, he or she might seek psychological treatment. A friend, spouse, or parent might refer someone for treatment. The individual might go see his primary care physician first and then be referred to a mental health practitioner.

Some people seek treatment because they are involved with the state's child protective services—that is, their children have been removed from their care due to abuse or neglect. The parents might be referred to psychiatric or substance abuse facilities and the children would likely receive treatment for trauma. If the parents are interested in and capable of becoming better parents, the goal of treatment might be family reunification. For other children whose parents are unable to change—for example, the parent or parents who are heavily addicted to drugs and refuse to enter treatment—the goal of therapy might be to help the children adjust to foster care and/or adoption.

Some people seek therapy because the criminal justice system referred them or required them to go. For some individuals, for example, attending weekly counseling sessions might be a condition of parole. If an individual is mandated to attend therapy, she is seeking services involuntarily. Involuntary treatment refers to therapy that is not the individual's choice. Other individuals might voluntarily seek treatment. Voluntary treatment means the person chooses to attend therapy to obtain relief from symptoms.

Psychological treatment can occur in a variety of places. An individual might go to a community mental health center or a practitioner in private or community practice. A child might see a school counselor, school psychologist, or school social worker. An incarcerated person might receive group therapy in prison. There are many different types of treatment providers, and licensing requirements vary from state to state. Besides psychologists and psychiatrists, there are clinical social workers, marriage and family therapists, and trained religious personnel who also perform counseling and therapy.

A range of funding sources pay for mental health treatment: health insurance, government, and private pay. In the past, even when people had health insurance, the coverage would not always pay for mental health services. This changed with the Mental Health Parity and Addiction Equity Act of 2008, which requires group health plans and insurers to make sure there is parity of mental health services. This means that co-pays, total number of visits, and deductibles for mental health and substance abuse treatment need to be equal to and cannot be more restrictive or harsher than those for physical illnesses and medical/surgical problems.

Finding treatment sources is also not always easy: there may be limited options, especially in rural areas and low-income urban areas; waiting lists; poor quality of care available for indigent patients; and financial obstacles such as co-pays, deductibles, and time off from work. Over 85% of the 1,669 federally designated mental health professional shortage areas are rural; often primary care physicians and law enforcement are the first-line mental health providers, although they do not have the specialized training of a mental health professional, who often would be better equipped to provide care. Availability, accessibility, and acceptability (the stigma attached to mental illness) are all problems in rural areas. Approximately two-thirds of those with symptoms receive no care at all. (At the end of 2013, the US Department of Agriculture announced an investment of $50 million to help improve access and treatment for mental health problems as part of the Obama administration's effort to strengthen rural communities.)

Summary

It was once believed that people with psychological disorders, or those exhibiting strange behavior, were possessed by demons. These people were forced to take part in exorcisms, were imprisoned, or executed. Later, asylums were built to house the mentally ill, but the patients received little to no treatment, and many of the methods used were cruel. Philippe Pinel and Dorothea Dix argued for more humane treatment of people with psychological disorders. In the mid-1960s, the deinstitutionalization movement gained support and asylums were closed, enabling people with mental illness to return home and receive treatment in their own communities. Some did go to their family homes, but many became homeless due to a lack of resources and support mechanisms.

Today, instead of asylums, there are psychiatric hospitals run by state governments and local community hospitals, with the emphasis on short-term stays. However, most people suffering from mental illness are not hospitalized. A person suffering symptoms could speak with a primary care physician, who most likely would refer him to someone who specializes in therapy. The person can receive outpatient mental health services from a variety of sources, including psychologists, psychiatrists, marriage and family therapists, school counselors, clinical social workers, and religious personnel. These therapy sessions would be covered through insurance, government funds, or private (self) pay.

New Efforts Are Being Made to Tear Down Barriers to Mental Health Care for Black Americans

Nina Bradley

Nina Bradley is a commerce writer for Bustle Digital Group. She previously wrote for Bustle's entertainment department.

On Tuesday, Aug. 13, *Empire* actor Taraji P. Henson revealed plans to launch a mental health foundation that will specially dedicate its efforts to helping the Black community, according to *Vibe*. The cause, while widespread, is one that strikes particularly close to home for Henson due to her own father's struggles with mental health which he faced following his discharge from the Vietnam War, according to the magazine.

The Boris Lawrence Henson Foundation, which Henson lovingly named in honor of her dad, will place distinct importance on changing the stigma of mental health for minorities, which has long affected people such as Henson's father. As part of its mission, the organization, which officially launches on September 22, will bring more understanding to the issue by providing scholarships to African-American students majoring in mental health while also offering mental wellness services to the youth in urban school districts.

When speaking to *People* about the foundation and its goals earlier this week, Henson shared her passion for the cause and revealed how her father, who died in 2006 at the age of 58 from liver cancer, became the inspiration for it all. She explained,

> "I named the organization after my father because of his complete and unconditional love for me; his unabashed, unashamed ability

"Taraji P. Henson's Black Mental Health Foundation Will Spread A Poignant Message With A Personal Connection," by Nina Bradley, Bustle Media Group, August 16, 2018. Reprinted by permission.

to tell the truth, even if it hurt; and his strength to push through his own battles with mental health issues."

The *Baby Boy* star went on to point out the trauma of being Black in America and pledged her support to make a change, explaining:

> "My dad fought in the Vietnam War for our country, returned broken, and received little to no physical and emotional support. I stand now in his absence, committed to offering support to African Americans who face trauma daily, simply because they are black."

By establishing the project in urban communities, it seems that Henson's foundation will place focus on where it's needed the most. Throughout history, there's been an overwhelmingly negative stigma—particularly within the Black community—related to mental health which often leads to apprehension when it comes to seeking out treatment. Those feelings of shame and guilt sometimes leave many in minority communities untreated, undiagnosed, and alone to deal with issues that require attention.

Hip-hop mogul JAY-Z has, in the past, used his platform to destigmatize the topic of therapy, something which he openly referred to in a *New York Times* interview as an experience that he "grew so much from." During a later sit down with CNN's Van Jones, the rapper shared the importance of therapeutic counseling, explaining:

> "As you grow, you realize the ridiculousness of the stigma attached to it. It's like, what? You just talk to someone about your problems."

He went on to say that he believes that there should be some sort of therapy integrated into the educational system that benefits children. Jay continued,

> "I think, actually, it should be in our schools. Children have the most going on…social anxiety and all these things are happening to you, and you don't have the language to navigate it."

The National Alliance on Mental Illness reveals that only about one-quarter of African-Americans seek out mental health care when it's needed, compared to 40 percent of white people. At the same time, NAMI points out that according to the Health and Human Services Office of Minority Health, African-Americans are actually 20 percent more likely to experience serious mental health issues than the general population.

It is not currently known why more African-Americans are stricken with mental health struggles. However, the fact that Blacks are far more likely to be the targets of violence may, perhaps, be at the root of the issue. *Essence* shares that in a series of federally funded studies in Atlanta, GA, where researchers interviewed more than 8,000 inner-city residents (most of them African-American), that two-thirds had encountered a violent attack in their lifetime. It also explains that half of those surveyed in the study knew someone who had been murdered. Out of the women who had been interviewed, one third revealed that they had been sexually assaulted. All-in-all, the study indicated that approximately 30 percent of the interviewees displayed symptoms consistent with Post-Traumatic Stress Disorder or PTSD, which *Essence* noted was at a rate just as high or higher than that of veterans who were in the wars in Vietnam, Iraq, and Afghanistan.

It's certainly a situation that deserves immediate attention and Henson appears to have good allies on her side. She's enlisted the help of her best friend Tracie Jenkins to serve as executive director of the foundation, according to *People*. Jenkins shared more detail on the organization's mission. Per *People*, she added:

> "BLHF is breaking the silence by speaking out and encouraging others to share their challenges with mental illness and get the help they need. African-Americans have regarded such communication as a sign of weakness and our vision is to change that perception."

Henson and Jenkins plan to kick off the project with a fundraising event called Taraji's Boutique of Hope on September 22 in Los Angeles, according to *People*. The outlet indicates that proceeds raised from the event will help to provide resources for the newly-minted foundation as it gets off the ground.

Henson's dedication to creating change in mental health and how it's perceived in the Black community is an inspiration and perhaps exactly what's needed to begin changing the public's view on therapy and mental well-being in general.

CHAPTER 4

Does Social Media Contribute to Americans' Mental Health Problems?

Social Media Has Both Advantages and Disadvantages for Mental Health

Jennifer Mattern

Jennifer Mattern is a professional blogger and freelance business writer who writes about social media issues for Social Implications.

I s the bite-sized world of social media leading to bite-sized and unsubstantial personal relationships? This was a question I asked myself recently when looking at some of my own relationships— friendship, romantic, professional, and family alike. Social media plays a role in many of those relationships these days, and what I noticed is that it isn't always for the better.

Today let's talk about how social media can inhibit the growth of deeper personal relationships with others, and then we'll take a look at the other side of the coin and how social media can play a positive role as well.

How Social Media Might Inhibit the Growth of Personal Relationships

Here's what I noticed when looking at my own relationships. Those that were heavily based in contact through social media outlets were much less substantial than those relationships where we kept in touch in person, over the phone, or via email on a regular basis. How those deeper relationships are maintained varied mostly based on physical distance.

For example, I have plenty of colleagues I consider friends. Many of them I keep in touch with solely through Twitter, social networks like LinkedIn, and blog comments. Those relationships tend to be much more casual, and we tend to know much less about each other. Once we hit the phase of emailing each other though, things change. Those relationships were much deeper

"Is Social Media Killing Personal Reltionships?" by Jennifer Mattern, Social Implications, February 21, 2011. Reprinted by permission.

than the social media based ones. We could have more private conversations. We could have *longer* conversations. And I found that people tended to open up much more about things unrelated to work via email than they did in social media.

The same was true with family. Those who keep in touch and work on maintaining a deeper personal connection generally turned to email, the phone, and in this case also snail mail. Those who only kept in touch via social media did so much more casually.

Sure, it's possible this is exclusive to me and my network of personal and professional connections. But for it to affect so many people and relationships in that network similarly leads me to think otherwise, although that's not to say there won't be exceptions. You see, social media makes it easy to get to the point and move on. And it makes it easy to provide so much "fluff" information that information overload results and you just don't *care* enough to want to know more mundane things about a person's life. So you don't reach deeper when communicating.

That might not be a bad thing on the professional side of things, but when it comes to more personal relationships I find it mildly concerning (and a good reason to make a better effort with friends and other loved ones). Do *you* reach out enough for the people you care about, or do you let social media suffice?

I do have to say that blogs are somewhat of an exception. They do give you a chance to get to know people better, because people can be as detailed as they want. However, that's mostly on the consumption side. Comments still are frequently brief compared to posts, limited to the scope of the post, and buried in a mass of other comments depending on the blog.

How Social Media Might *Improve* Personal Relationships

Now that's not to say that I think social media is killing personal relationships really. The only ones who can do that are ourselves if we slack off and stop making a decent effort just because social media is "easier." In fact, I do think social media can do positive things in helping to build relationships—especially new ones.

Most importantly, I think social media tools have the ability to serve as a stepping stone to deeper and more personal relationships with those we want to build them with. For example, I'd known a particular freelance writing colleague for a while. And I knew she lived just a few towns over. We got to know each other mostly through blogs, but also kept in touch occasionally through Twitter. Because of that, we later met in person a couple of times. And at *that* point we really took the time to get to know each other better on a more personal level—discussing family, local shops, and such rather than solely work. In that case I like to think of social media as a sort of extended introduction.

The More Time People Spend on Social Media, the Less Happy They Are

Gigen Mammoser

Gigen Mammoser is a Los Angeles-based journalist who has worked as an editor for Vice Media and founded Inane Media, which serves clients such as Vice and Healthline.

No matter what you did today on your phone or computer, it's likely that social media was involved.

Did you catch up with friends on Facebook, post photos of your dog on Instagram? Maybe a Twitter link brought you here.

In the United States today, you're statistically more likely to use social media than not—by a lot. Approximately 77 percent of all Americans have a social media profile of some kind.

Despite the popularity of social media platforms and the rapidity with which they've inserted themselves into nearly all facets of our lives, there's a remarkable lack of clear data about how they affect us personally: our behaviors, our social relationships, and our mental health.

In many cases, the information that's available isn't pretty.

Studies have linked the use of social media to depression, anxiety, poorer sleep quality, lower self-esteem, inattention, and hyperactivity—often in teens and adolescents.

The list goes on.

However, these studies are almost entirely of an observational or correlational nature, meaning they don't establish whether or not one is causing the other.

A common argument against the theory that social media makes individuals more depressed and lonely is simply that perhaps those who are more depressed and lonely are more inclined to use social media as a way of reaching out.

"The FOMO Is Real: How Social Media Increases Depression and Loneliness," by Gigen Mammoser, Healthline Media, December 9, 2018. Reprinted by permission.

Does Social Media Cause Depression?

A new study concludes that there is in fact a causal link between the use of social media and negative effects on well-being, primarily depression and loneliness. The study was published in the *Journal of Social and Clinical Psychology.*

"What we found overall is that if you use less social media, you are actually less depressed and less lonely, meaning that the decreased social media use is what causes that qualitative shift in your well-being," said Jordyn Young, a co-author of the paper and a senior at the University of Pennsylvania.

"Prior to this, all we could say was that there is an association between using social media and having poor outcomes with well-being," she said.

The researchers say this is the first time a causal link has ever been established in scientific research.

The study included 143 students from the University of Pennsylvania. They were randomly assigned to one of two groups: one that would continue their social media habits as usual or one that would significantly limit access to social media.

For three weeks, the experimental group had their social media use reduced to 30 minutes per day—10 minutes on three different platforms (Facebook, Instagram, and Snapchat).

In order to keep these experimental conditions, the researchers looked at phone usage data, which documented how much time was spent using each app per day. All of the study participants had to use iPhones.

But why even let the experimental group use social media at all?

"We didn't think [complete abstinence] was an accurate representation of the landscape of the world that we live in today. Social media is around us in so many capacities," Young said.

The results were clear: The group that used less social media, even though it wasn't completely eliminated, had better mental health outcomes.

Baseline readings for participants were taken at the beginning of the trial in several areas of well-being: social support, fear of missing out, loneliness, anxiety, depression, self-esteem, autonomy, and self-acceptance.

At the end of the trial, those in the experimental group saw both loneliness and depressive symptoms decline, with the largest changes happening in those who reported greater levels of depression.

"No matter where they started off, if they were told to limit their social media, they had less depression, no matter what their initial levels were," Young said.

Meanwhile, both groups saw a decline in levels of anxiety and fear of missing out, which the researchers posit as potentially coming from users simply becoming more aware of their social media use by taking part in the trial.

Even with an established causal link, there still remains a larger, unanswered question: Why?

Our Curated Lives

How could systems designed to bring us closer to our friends and family be bad for our mental health?

Much like the algorithm that powers your Facebook feed, it's complicated.

Some general theories have come to the forefront, some obvious and some not so much.

"What happens many times when they log on is that you kind of activate a lot of social comparison," said Oscar Ybarra, PhD, a professor of psychology at the University of Michigan. "People don't necessarily have to be super aware that this is occurring, but it does. You log on, you're generally dealing with very curated content on the other side."

Ybarra has published pieces on the relationship between Facebook and certain mental health outcomes. He's attempted to suss out the "why" of this relationship for himself.

He notes that even if individuals are aware of the "curated" nature of many online platforms, "they nevertheless feel like, 'How am I stacking up?' or 'How is my life stacking up?' compared to what these people are presenting. I think that what happens is that the more you use the platforms, the more social comparisons tend to induce, and that relates to these decrements in how people are feeling."

These constant "upward social comparisons" can happen hundreds of times each day, depending on how frequently you check your social media feeds.

The FOMO Is Real

Fear of missing out, or FOMO, is another mental health effect that's been strongly linked with the use of social media.

Although a relatively new phrase often attributed to millennial ennui, psychologists say it has real social significance.

Amy Summerville, PhD, a professor of psychology at Miami University in Ohio, is an expert on issues of regret and the psychology of "what might have been."

She explains that FOMO is an extension of larger issues of inclusion and social standing.

Once our basic needs are met, like food, shelter, and water, the need for inclusion and social interaction ranks right up there, she says.

"The FOMO experience specifically is this feeling that I personally could have been there and I wasn't. I do think that part of the reason that's really powerful is this cue that maybe we're not being included by people we have important social relationships with," she told Healthline.

The now ubiquitous use of social media and technology has created a world in which we can gaze into our own crystal ball to see what our friends are doing at almost any time of day. And that's not necessarily a good thing.

So, should we all just be using less social media?

Maybe. But both Ybarra and Summerville say there isn't enough research to set any kind of real guidelines.

"I don't know that I would say, at this point, that the research necessarily says that everyone needs to put app blockers on their phone," Summerville said. "It does, to me, suggest that this could be helpful, especially for people who are already seeming to struggle with negative emotions and a sense of belonging."

Nevertheless, what's clear is that social media isn't going away. If anything, this kind of technology will likely only grow more pervasive.

Games like "Pokémon Go" changed the social atmosphere of what it means to play a video game. Apps like Strava have created a social network where users can share their fitness goals and routines. And LinkedIn has gone from a job-hunting platform to a full-on social network for the career-minded.

"Given how available these technologies are and continue to become, they are just going to be part of how we interact with our world and with people. There's definitely a lot of work to be done in this area," Ybarra said.

The Bottom Line

Social media use can harm your mental health, especially when it's used more frequently.

Setting limits and sticking to them can help minimize these effects.

Social Media Can Make Difficult Times Feel Even Worse

Hannah Blum

Hannah Blum is a writer and mental health advocate who has chronicled her life as a young woman living with bipolar II disorder on her blog, Halfway2Hannah. She has a bachelor's degree in communications and media studies from North Carolina State University.

I am not a relationship expert, but I've had my heart broken more than I'd like to admit. On this journey in heartbreak, I realized that a significant part of emotionally surviving a breakup is to take a break from anything that could be toxic in your environment, including social media. No, you do not have to delete everything or go into hibernation, but you do have to stay off them as much as possible and take the initiative to block or unfollow your ex to prevent you from seeing their posts. It relates to the old saying, *"Out of sight out of mind."*

Get Off Social Media? What Kind of Sick Suggestion Is This?

Trust me; I am not anti-social media or someone who believes it's destroying humanity. It's the opposite. I am a blogging millennial with a pro-social media stance. However, I am not naive to the harm it can have on a person's mental health. Social media connects us to everyone, including people we are "supposed" to move on from at some point.

Think about it like a physical wound. If you don't allow yourself to heal, you only do more damage. A broken heart is an internal wound, and social media keeps that wound open and exposed. After a breakup, we torture ourselves by staying connected to our ex

"How to Mentally Survive a Breakup: Stay Off Social Media," by Hannah Blum, HALFWAY2HANNAH, April 12, 2018. Reprinted by permission.

via social media. We check to see whose pics they liked, who they are following and analyze every new post on their feed. It gives us a false sense of hope that we may still be relevant to our ex-lover. Snapchat views, Instagram and Facebook "Likes" suddenly translates as he or she may still have romantic feelings. We inflict emotional and mental pain on ourselves. It keeps us from shutting a door that is desperately waiting to be slammed shut.

I highly doubt you have ever heard someone going through a breakup say, "Following him on Instagram has given me closure." It's more along the lines of, "Did you see his post the other day…" It's a constant reminder that we are not with the person we once loved, which makes us more insecure.

When Do I Get Back on Social Media After a Breakup?

Let's say you read this post while you're going through a terrible breakup. You take my advice and tell yourself that you will keep off social media for 30 days. You do it, and on day 31 you grab your phone and open up Instagram. If one of the first things you do is unblock your ex or search their username @ personthatbrokeyourheart, you are not ready. It's like going on a diet for 30 days, and on day 31 you go back to eating junk food. What happens? You gain all the weight back and probably feel even worse. When you don't feel the need to use social media to connect or check up on your ex-lover, then take a selfie and announce your social comeback. #ImBackBetch.

Following your ex, or someone who romantically rejected you, on social media has no benefits, so why do it? You are traveling on a road that leads to a dead end. Social media is meant to share epic moments and periods of our lives with those who deserve it. Breakups suck, but guess what? You are going to be okay, and you are going to find a love that will make you look back at your exes and think, "Holy sh*t what the f*ck was I thinking!" I can't wait for you to find that type of love. Social media isn't going anywhere don't worry!

Narcissism Is a Part of Daily Life Due to Social Media

W. Keith Campbell

Dr. W. Keith Campbell is a professor of psychology at the University of Georgia and an author of numerous books and articles on narcissism, including When You Love a Man Who Loves Himself: How to Deal with a One-Way Relationship.

There has been a massive increase in the use of social media—from being almost non-existent 15 years ago, it now takes up a major part of our lives and our children's lives.

Facebook, for example, boasts over one billion users per day.

This explosion of social media has led to many cultural, social, and economic changes.

Narcissism—having an inflated view of oneself—has become a major topic of research interest, and also of concern.

Is social media becoming an outlet for narcissistic individuals to self-promote? And is social media turning us and our children into narcissists?

Seeking Attention

Some use their social media accounts as platforms for self-promotion—places to seek attention and admiration. Others take up an oversized amount of space in social media feeds.

These "friends" bragging about their amazing lives—replete with pictures and hashtags—come across as at least a bit narcissistic.

Even the names and taglines of many social media sites seemed to reflect this narcissistic, or at least individualistic, bent.

Youtube: "broadcast yourself." Twitter: "what are you doing?"; and "iPod," "iPad" and "iPhone."

Time magazine named "You" the person of the year in 2006, and even included a mirror and computer on the cover.

Facebook was named after the books some schools publish with everyone's name and face. And LinkedIn was designed for business networking (the "links").

This led to culture becoming considerably more self-focused.

Hardware designers made cameras that took pictures of their owners, and the selfie took over. Selfie was named word of the year by the Oxford English Dictionary in 2013. (The first use of the word "selfie" was actually by a drunk Aussie in 2002 who took a picture of his own bloodied lip after a fall to show his friends.)

Today we have 100 million people on social media sites like Snapchat taking selfies, running them through filters, and sending them to friends.

Researchers follow these trends as best they can, but they are always about two years behind.

Narcissists Are More Self-Promoting

A 2008 study on narcissism and Facebook found evidence that more narcissistic individuals were more self-promoting on Facebook and had more "friends."

This finding is consistent with what many people expect—narcissistic individuals do well in an environment where there are shallow relationships and opportunities to self-promote.

It does not mean that Facebook is only for narcissism—social media is a tool that can be used to form and maintain close relationships, learn new things, or just provide entertainment. But it is also an attractive place for narcissists to do their thing.

This finding has held up across many other studies across the world, with narcissism predicting self-promotion and number of connections.

More recently, researchers have tackled the question of narcissism and selfies.

Several papers have found that narcissistic individuals take more selfies, spend more time on social media, feel good about it, and are a little more self-promoting (for example, show more body shots and more solo selfies).

They also tend to be well integrated into these social media networks, having large numbers of friends and followers. In general, men are a little more narcissistic than women, but we find that narcissistic men and women use social media in similar ways.

Does Social Media Increase Narcissism?

The more challenging question is if the arrow points the other way. That is, does social media use cause narcissism?

This has proven a much more challenging question to answer. When we first studied changes in narcissism over time, it looked like narcissism and social media use might be accelerating together.

But this data is correlational and doesn't tell us about individuals' social media use; therefore it doesn't really say much about how social media will influence users.

Since then, researchers have tried a couple different strategies.

One is experimental. For example, you take two random groups, have one group work on their social media page and the other on an unrelated computer task. Then you measure differences in narcissism to see if the social media group is higher. Results from this approach have been mixed and inconclusive.

Another approach is longitudinal, measuring narcissism and social media use over time and seeing if they are mutually reinforcing; that is, whether narcissism predicts increased social media use and whether that, in turn, predicts increasing narcissism. At least one study shows this pattern.

It might also be the case that social media inflates the narcissism of those already predisposed, but has no effect on others.

So it is plausible that social media use increases narcissism. But there is also longitudinal research suggesting that social media use can make children more empathetic. For example, children who spend time engaged with their friends on social media might become more concerned with the up and downs in their friends' lives.

Thus, given the vagaries of social science and the challenge of figuring out how to answer the causal question (without randomly assigning 300 children to avoid social media until they turn 18 and have their narcissism measured), I think it is best to wait for more data.

Successful Social Media Creators

Narcissists are successful social media creators. They build bridges to others and generate content. They may be annoying at times and have a small risk for Internet addiction, but the role that narcissistic individuals play in building social media networks may have helped create the massive social media we have today.

Social Media Isn't to Blame for Mental Disorders Like Narcissism

Lisa Firestone

Lisa Firestone, PhD, is the director of research and education at the Glendon Association, which advocates for mental health by addressing common social problems. She speaks at conferences around the world to discuss couple relations, parenting, suicide, and violence prevention. She has published numerous articles and books, including The Self Under Siege *and* Sex and Love in Intimate Relationships.

Studies are now showing what many of you may have suspected: We are living in an increasingly narcissistic society.

In a world where prime-time television is dominated by a "reality" as false as the Kardashians' lashes, and people sit across dinner tables checking in on Facebook rather than having face-to-face conversations, this may not come as a surprise.

Much has been written about the rise of narcissism amongst millennials, the generation born in the 1980s and 1990s, a generation controversially dubbed "Generation Me" by Professor Jean M. Twenge in 2007. In her most recent work, *The Narcissistic Epidemic: Living in the Age of Entitlement*, Twenge (with W. Keith Campbell) explains: "In data from 37,000 college students, narcissistic personality traits rose just as fast as obesity from the 1980s to the present." The comparison to obesity suggests that narcissism is another epidemic in America.

Perhaps more troubling, a handful of new studies comparing traits and life goals of young people in high school and college today with those of Gen-Xers and baby boomers at the same age, show an increase in extrinsic values rather than intrinsic values. Millennials are more likely to value money, image and fame over community, affiliation and self-acceptance.

"Is Social Media to Blame for the Rise in Narcissism?" by Lisa Firestone, PhD, PsychAlive. Reprinted by permission.

So who's to blame for this generational increase in narcissism?

Can we pin the tail on Mark Zuckerberg and the advent of Facebook? Over the last couple years, a plethora of research has been pouring in that makes connections between Facebook and narcissism. Studies are consistently finding that people who score higher on the Narcissistic Personality Inventory questionnaire tend to have more friends on Facebook, tag themselves more often in photos and update their statuses more frequently. According to Laura Buffadi, a postdoctoral researcher at the Universidad de Dueto in Bilbao, Spain, "Narcissists use Facebook and other social networking sites because they believe others are interested in what they're doing, and they want others to know what they are doing."

In general, social media websites encourage self-promotion, as users generate all of the content. W. Keith Campbell explains that people often utilize Facebook "to look important, look special and to gain attention and status and self-esteem." The trouble with this aspect of social networking is that nearly everyone presents an unrealistic portrait of themselves. Just as people select the most attractive photos of themselves to use as profile pictures, they tend to populate their newsfeeds with the most attractive bits of news about themselves. Of course, this is not always the case, but the unrealistically sunny picture that so many social networkers paint can have a negative psychological effect on their friends or followers. Recent studies of undergraduates across the country have shown that "students who were more involved with Facebook were more likely to think other people's lives were happier and better." These heavy Facebook users were also more likely to negatively compare themselves to others and feel worse about themselves.

While Facebook is certainly a platform for narcissists, it is a mistake to assume that Facebook alone has caused this spike in narcissism. As researcher Shawn Bergman pointed out, "There is a significant amount of psychological research that shows that one's personality is fairly well-established by age 7," given that Facebook's policy doesn't allow users to register until age 13 "the personality traits of typical users are fairly well-ingrained by the time they get on a social network."

The truth is the rise in narcissism among millennials may have less to do with our social networks online and more to do with our social networks at home. Throughout the last few decades, there has been an increase in parental coddling and the so-called "self-esteem" movement. Parents and teachers trying to instill a healthy sense of self-esteem in children by praising them lavishly often do more harm than good. In fact, studies show that children offered compliments for a skill they have not mastered or talents that they do not have are left feeling emptier and more insecure. Only when children are praised for real accomplishments are they able to build actual self-esteem.

I have written previously about the fundamental differences of self-esteem vs. narcissism:

> Self-esteem differs from narcissism in that it represents an attitude built on accomplishments we've mastered, values we've adhered to, and care we've shown toward others. Narcissism, conversely, is often based on a fear of failure or weakness, a focus on one's self, an unhealthy drive to be seen as the best, and a deep-seated insecurity and underlying feeling of inadequacy.

It is important to understand that narcissism stems from underlying feelings of inadequacy. Many children of the millennial generation were given form rather than substance, presents instead of presence, which leaves children feeling insecure. Empty praise causes children to feel entitled while lacking the true confidence necessary to feel good about themselves. Our society's shift towards instant gratification appears to be having a negative effect on our kids.

In our recent book *The Self Under Siege*, my father Dr. Robert Firestone and I write about the importance of parents encouraging their children to have a true sense of self. In order for children to feel secure and confident in themselves, it is essential for parents to distinguish emotional hunger from real love. Real parental love includes warmth, affection and attunement to a child's needs, as well as offering the child guidance, direction and control when appropriate. This type of love helps children develop real self-esteem rather than narcissistic personality traits.

While it is certain that online forms of communication and social networks do affect individual's mental health, the solution to fostering a less narcissistic generation is to instill a healthy sense of true esteem offline before anyone is old enough to post their first status update. Only by being less self-obsessed and placing more value on personal relating can we impart these values to the next generation.

Users Can Get the Best Out of Social Media By Using It Wisely

Alex Perekalin

Alex Perekalin is a content strategist for Kaspersky Lab in Moscow, Russia. Kapersky Lab runs a blog about cybersecurity and technology.

Not long ago, I finished reading a book by Johann Hari called *Lost Connections*, which I absolutely recommend to anyone who feels even slightly depressed or anxious. It is a very, very good book that urges people to reconnect with normal human relationships, meaningful values, and doing something that matters—trust me, that can really help overcome depression. It's not a universal antidote to distress, but it can at least give you an understanding of the nebulous reasons you're feeling unhappy.

What struck me while I was reading the book is that some of the things Hari pointed out about our broken society and ways to fix it are also related to our privacy. Actually, it's quite surprising, yet it really seems that taking care of your online privacy can have a positive impact on your mental state. In this rather personal post I would like to describe two aspects of privacy that are quite directly related to feeling morally well. I would like to note that I'm speaking on my personal behalf, and the official position of the company might be different.

Social Networks: The Disconnection from Other People

It's a paradox of the modern world: Social networks allow us to talk with our friends and relatives all over the globe at any time, yet never in human history have we felt so lonely and disconnected from others.

"Why Online Privacy Is Good for Our Mental Health," by Alex Perekalin, AO Kaspersky Lab, October 11, 2018. Reprinted by permission.

That disconnect is something pointed out not only by Hari, but also by a lot of different, independent sources, including our own survey. Social networks cannot serve as a replacement for normal, real-life communication with people you value. Even in terms of chemicals, communicating over social networks is different from talking with a flesh-and-blood human face to face; in the latter case, a hormone called oxytocin is released, and it (together with serotonin and dopamine) is responsible for us feeling happy.

We've talked a lot about privacy and security in social networks on our blog, suggesting changing the settings for Facebook, LinkedIn, Twitter, Instagram, and so on. Most of these changes aim to prevent strangers from seeing information they shouldn't. We've also talked about the habit of oversharing and its negative consequences. But the more I dug into social media privacy settings and the more I read about data leaking from social networks (be it a Cambridge Analytica scandal, or, say, an Ashley Madison leak), the more I thought about the idea of not having social media accounts at all—or at least minimizing my time on social networks.

I'm not a person who jumps to do something as soon as I hear about it, so I've been considering this idea a lot, and I've come to the following conclusion: I won't delete my Facebook, Twitter, LinkedIn, and other social accounts. They are all good for something. Facebook serves me birthday reminders, and it's helped me communicate with former journalist colleagues or acquaintances when I needed information from them for my posts here. LinkedIn is probably good for my career (at least that's what people say; I haven't had a chance to try it for myself, although it helped me find career opportunities for my wife). Twitter is a social network used by a lot of information security researchers, and it is a good source of news in our industry.

For me, the solution is to set social networks' privacy settings to be as strict as possible, minimize my time on them, and not consider them a way to communicate with friends and relatives. And I deleted Instagram and Swarm, which were constantly making me feel miserable and envious of other people. After applying these changes and spending significantly less time scrolling through the feeds, I've found myself feeling less miserable and having more time to actually see my friends, which makes me feel even better.

It's a personal solution that worked for me and might not be right for you, but I want you to at least ask yourself: Do you really need all those accounts in all those social networks, and do you really need to spend that much time checking them? Minimizing communication and sharing on social networks is a way to increase your online privacy and to feel better. Deleting your account might work even better—if you are ready for that radical step.

Advertising: The Disconnection from Meaningful Values

It is believed that we are exposed to an average of more than 4,000 ads per day. We don't consciously notice all of them, but there they are: billboards on the street, banners on websites, text ads on search engines, promoted posts on social networks, and so on. Not to mention that many people wear clothes advertising brands. The modern world wants us all to buy things, and hundreds of thousands of very talented marketers and salespeople work daily to make us believe that buying this or that brand new thing will make us happier, or better, or help us achieve our dreams.

Perhaps there is some truth to that—for example, buying a bike might make you happier because of the joy that going for a ride can bring. But buying a new, expensive, and super-mega-feature-packed bike instead of an older, plainer one won't make you significantly happier; the rides in the park will be almost the same. A fancy new bike might raise your standing among people on the street, but it doesn't matter to the people who really care about you.

Yet ads urge us to buy more and more fancy new stuff. No matter what kind of car you have, there's always a car that packs more horsepower and provides more features. And personalized ads will urge you to take a look at it, perhaps try it so that you'll really want to have it. Personalized ads that we see in search engines and social networks are the heaviest hitters, because they are tailored specifically for us. But the things they promote are not what we really want, they are what our society wants us to want. These are called *extrinsic values*; our real values are called *intrinsic*.

Our intrinsic values are usually not about having, but about doing (say, learning to play a musical instrument) or caring. They're about doing meaningful things for the people we care about or for society in general. Sometimes, they're about becoming something.

Pursuing our intrinsic values—the ideas that really matter to us—is one of the things that makes us happy, makes us want to live our life. But intrinsic values are often hidden, overshadowed by extrinsic ones because no one advertises our intrinsic values to us—our quest is to dig into ourselves and find them. Extrinsic values are advertised on every site or corner. And on the Internet the ads are, once again, tailored specifically to hook us.

What information is used to make online ads relevant? It is our posts on social media, our likes, our geographical positioning data, the things we've searched. It is what we write in our Gmail and what we talk about on Facebook Messenger. It is what is now called *big data*.

How do we avoid targeted ads? By not giving too much information to those who serve them and by not allowing them to track us. Hello again, privacy.

Well, I'm not talking about dropping Gmail for good—it's too convenient. I use it and plan on continuing to use it. But again, this post is about starting to think about which services that you use and that collect your data for advertising purposes are really necessary, and which of them can be easily replaced with more privacy-oriented ones.

I've described my approach to social media; now, it's up to you to develop yours. Minimizing time on social media means you'll see fewer ads and give away less personal data that can be used to target you. But there are search engines and, say, news websites that also want to serve you customized ads. You can avoid that by using software that prevents tracking and services that are pro-privacy. For example, I recently switched from using Google as a search engine to privacy-oriented Web-search platform DuckDuckGo. It still serves ads, because that's how it earns money, but it does not track you and does not have a gigantic advertising network such as Google Ads, which means that other sites won't be serving you ads based on your searches.

The Results

Having more time to talk in person with people who matter and fewer ads to clutter my brain did a good job for me and, perhaps, it might do a good job for you. For me, it resulted in finding out that there are people around me who have the same problems as I, and solving them together—or at least sharing them—made those problems seem significantly smaller and more bearable.

Perhaps, I can say that after reading Hari's book and making some tweaks in my life I'm a happier person than I used to be, and the process aligned really nicely with my idea of increasing my privacy online. And as a part of reconnecting with meaningful values, I want to create something that has at least a chance to make other people's lives better. That's why I'm writing this post, and I really hope it can help at least some of you.

Social Media Has Positive and Negative Aspects, and It's Up to Users to Decide What They Do with It

Chomwa Shikati

Chomwa Shikati is an entrepreneur, accountant, and writer who serves as editor for What It Takes. *He is based in Zambia.*

Does anyone still remember a world without social media? It is hard to believe that only a little over a decade ago, our way of life was really different from the way it is now.

Although there were some social media sites long before that, most of the population did not really see the need or use for it. Most did not even have the access to them. It wasn't until Facebook, Twitter and smart phones came along when things really started to change.

Needless to say that in 2017, social media has forever changed the way society works, whether it's the sharing of an idea, the communication of news, or the availability of a product or service. Social media is now used in almost every part of our lives.

I am not a huge fan of social media myself, partly because I prefer to live life in the real world, and partly because am naturally a private individual. And yet here I am, using social media to let you hear my opinion on social media.

The benefits of social media are very hard to ignore.

What are some ways social media has changed the way we do things?

Business Impact

Businesses across the globe can now amplify their brand message to a wider audience than they could ever dream of doing before achieving success that they could only wish for. In the old days,

"Ways Social Media Has Changed Our Society," by Chomwa Shikati, What It Takes, November 9, 2017. Reprinted by permission.

mass media ruled. A company had to pony up thousands or even millions of dollars to be heard in most cases. Very large companies with deep pockets ruled the roost. Only those businesses could afford to have wider reach.

And now?

Well, even an individual with a very brilliant idea coupled with excellent marketing abilities can achieve great financial success on social media.

Small companies are carving out a market for themselves amongst the 2.4 billion people estimated to be connected on social media quite easily. Compared to television advertisements and other expensive forms of marketing, social media presence is a cheap and effective means to enhance brand image and popularity.

Social media has moved from a "nice to have" to a "must have" component or department of a company's business strategy.

Social media has also changed how businesses recruit individuals into their companies. Looking back to 10 years ago, recruiters were limited in the ways they could reach out and engage with potential candidates and clients, but thanks to the rise of the internet and mobile devices paired with the growth of social media, it would seem modern day recruiters are now spoilt for choice in the ways they can make contact with potential candidates and clients.

Social Impact

In terms of social circles, social media has broken down barriers when it comes to communicating and we are spoilt for choice when it comes to ways of getting in contact with someone.

Social media has also made it easier for us to express ourselves. There are numerous ways we can express ourselves, not only to our friends but to the outside world. Whether that is through Facebook, Instagram pictures, YouTube videos, Medium articles. Normal people now have the capacity to make their opinion known on a massive scale. Before social media, you could have an opinion but you could only tell a few people close to you, and now, the story is different. Within a few minutes, thousands could know about your opinion.

Social media has also made it easier for us to track people down. I know what some of my former high school peers are up to even when I have not even been in touch with some of them for years. It's that easy. There are seemingly endless sources we can search to access the information we need to find the people we have to find.

Social networks offer the opportunity for people to re-connect with their old friends and acquaintances, make new friends, trade ideas, share content and pictures, and many other activities.

But just like most things, there are drawbacks and downsides to the excessive use and reliance of social media…

First of all, the idea of "friends" was once very simple. If you knew someone, hung out with them regularly, and liked their company then they were a friend. While the people who still fit that description are still your friends, so are the people you have connected with on social networking sites apparently. Whether you talk to them, care about what they're up to, or have any interest in them whatsoever, they're still listed as friends.

Quite too often you see people with double identities. A self-centred attitude and the need to be accepted and liked by 'friends' on social media has led people to create or lead a life that they feel will be accepted and liked by the masses. And well most people attach their self-esteem to their social media activity.

Another thing that most people forget, is that, if you are not careful, what you post on the Net can come back to haunt you. Revealing personal information on social sites can make users vulnerable to crimes like identity theft, stalking, etc. As stated earlier on, many companies perform a background check on the Internet before hiring an employee. If a prospective employee has posted something embarrassing on social media, it can drastically affect their chances of getting the job.

In terms of productivity, it is quite easy to lose your focus on what you're doing because of being addicted to social media. In fact, many companies have blocked social networks on their office Internet as addicted employees can distract themselves on such sites, instead of focusing on work.

Cyber bullying is also becoming frequent. If you are not careful, unscrupulous people can target you for cyber bullying and harassment on social sites. School children, young girls, and women can fall prey to online attacks which can create tension and distress.

Conclusion

No doubt that social media is changing and will continue to change our society. This change is permanent because the upcoming generation won't even know a world where social media does not exist. This has its advantages and disadvantages, but like everything else, it's up to the user to decide whether social media can enhance their lives or not and this all depends on how they decide to use it.

Social Media Can Be Used to Facilitate Mental Health Interventions

Brad Ridout and Andrew Campbell

Dr. Brad Ridout is a child and adolescent psychologist and a cyberpsychology and digital health researcher. He is part of the University of Sydney Cyberpsychology Research Group. Dr. Andrew Campbell is the lead academic in the Cyberpsychology Research Group and is a senior lecturer in psychology at the University of Sydney.

Supporting the mental health of young people is a major public health challenge, with mental disorders accounting for almost half of the nonfatal burden of disease among people aged 10 to 25 years. Adolescence is a particularly vulnerable period of development, with the onset of mental health problems peaking between adolescence and young adulthood. However, many problems are not detected until later in life, as young people are often reluctant to seek professional help and face barriers to treatment such as cost, poor mental health literacy, confidentiality concerns, stigma, and inaccessibility to or lack of knowledge of resources.

Given that internet-enabled mobile devices have become a near-ubiquitous element of adolescence, with 45% of teens admitting that they are online *almost constantly*, it is not surprising that young people are increasingly seeking support and information regarding their mental health online.

Over the past decade, social media has become an important element of communication for young people, with virtually all having at least one active social media account. People with mental illness are often among the highest users, with many reporting that social media fosters community among users and makes them feel supported and accepted. Furthermore, a recent study found that actively engaging with peers online about their mental health concerns was associated with an increased likelihood of seeking formal mental health care.

Social networking sites (SNSs), a subset of social media, have become the predominant context for communication and social support–seeking behaviors online among adolescents. SNS users create a profile within a bounded system, which they use to make and display connections with other users. Posting of user-generated and Web-based content and functions such as liking, commenting, and tagging are the lifeblood of SNSs and differentiate SNSs from Web 1.0 communication tools such as message boards and online support groups.

Given the barriers to mental health support young people face and the fact that they are naturally turning to SNSs to engage in knowledge seeking and peer-to-peer support, there is a promising opportunity to use SNSs to deliver or integrate with youth-focused online mental health interventions. Compared with other online mental health resources such as online counseling, mobile apps, and online support groups, research into the use of SNSs to support and treat young people with mental health issues is only in its infancy and is highly fragmented. Although there have been reviews evaluating the effectiveness of SNSs for specific mental health disorders in young people and online peer-to-peer support for young people more broadly, none of the reviews have covered the breadth of SNS-based youth mental health interventions available across all mental health issues. A systematic review of the literature regarding the use of SNS-based interventions to support the mental health of young people is, therefore, required to evaluate their effectiveness, suitability, and safety and identify gaps and opportunities for future research.

[…]

Discussion

Principal Findings

The aim of this systematic review was to identify studies investigating the use of SNS to support the mental health of children and youth. A total of 9 articles reporting on 5 separate studies were identified. Of the 9 studies, 2 studies targeted specific mental health issues (depression and psychosis), whereas the other studies focused on improving mental health literacy, social support, and general well-being. Only 3 quantitative studies were identified and all used a pre-post design (without a control group) to establish *proof of concept*, rather than causal inferences about efficacy. Although this precluded any meta-analysis or assessment using Effective Practice and Organization of Care quality criteria, some of the outcome measures produced encouraging results, with significant reductions in depressive symptoms and significant improvements in mental health knowledge. However, there was no significant reduction in anxiety or psychosis symptoms. Acceptability and usability of the platforms reviewed were generally high, as were perceptions of usefulness and safety. There were no adverse incidents reported in any of the studies. When offered a choice, users showed a preference for mobile apps over Web-based interfaces and appreciated receiving notification alerts on their mobile phones. Overall, this review found evidence for the potential for SNS-based interventions to support the mental health of young people.

Engagement with the SNS platforms was high in most studies, with low dropout rates, and most users logging in and actively posting and engaging with content, moderators, and other users, on at least a weekly basis. Moderation was identified as a key component of the success of the interventions. The therapeutic interventions that were most favorably viewed by users were those that were guided by moderators within the social networking environment, with users generally finding moderators to be friendly, supportive, and caring. There was also initial support for the inclusion of peer moderators to act as role models and support the experience of other users; however, it is not suggested that these should replace the role of expert moderators with clinical experience.

Positive feedback on the benefit of giving and receiving peer-to-peer support was also received, consistent with established literature. Users of the MOST [moderated online social therapy] platforms reported that the most valued characteristic of the intervention was the ability to connect with other young people of a similar age with shared experiences, backgrounds, and mental health issues. Users felt safe because the sites could only be accessed by clients of the mental health services from which they had been recruited, which also contributed to feelings of belonging to a group of peers with similar experiences. There were indications that users felt understood, supported, more socially connected, and more willing to discuss their issues as a result of interacting with peers who were facing challenges similar to them.

However, not all users were active in their use of the social networking functions, with qualitative feedback revealing that some users preferred to *eavesdrop* on discussions taking place or *lurk*. Olga Santesteban-Echarri et al. identified 2 clear subgroups of low interactors in the Rebound study. The first subgroup did not like online interaction and/or had sufficient offline support, supporting the typology of social media users by Gillian Fergie et al. that suggests the more offline support someone has, the less regularly they engage with health-related content on social media. The second subgroup of low interactors simply felt too shy, indicating that either the activity on the site was not high enough for them to feel comfortable to initiate a conversation or that not *knowing* fellow users was a barrier (despite anonymity being one of the obvious advantages and aims of closed SNSs for supporting youth mental health). This desire to know other users was also raised by participants in the YBMen project, who suggested that having occasional face-to-face meetings would have benefited the intervention (although the authors note that this may have been influenced by the project's association with an existing offline group).

Although it is possible that having a less than positive regard for anonymous online interactions may be a potential barrier to gaining benefit from SNS-based youth mental health interventions, more research is needed to establish whether eavesdropping on discussions may still be beneficial for low interactors. Recent research suggests that having a strong sense of community and inclusive culture are important factors for deriving positive outcomes among lurkers of online health support groups. The design of SNSs for supporting youth mental health should, therefore, engage in strategies to create a sense of community and promote regular contributions from users, given it appears that variable levels of interactivity and engagement over time are features of these platforms.

Overall, the integration of the social networking components with the psychoeducation and therapy modules in the MOST interventions was considered successful, as evidenced by a high level of engagement with both and positive qualitative feedback from users. The MindMax and Ching Ching Story platforms also aimed to integrate social networking functions with the online education activities around mental health literacy, for example, by encouraging users to post about their successes in completing activities and comment on the successes of others. However, there was no evidence provided to suggest that the social networking functions were well utilized during the trials of these 2 platforms (although it was stated that *social connectedness* of MindMax users will be reported in a future evaluation of a naturalistic trial).

The need to integrate therapeutic and social networking functions was not an issue for the YBMen project, as all activities took place within the closed Facebook group. This had the additional benefit of locating the intervention within a platform that most users were already familiar with and using daily on multiple devices, including mobile devices, which was something that users appreciated. Although using naturally occurring SNS such as Facebook to deliver interventions could be a way to address the difficulty that purpose-built platforms may face in creating the norms, dynamics, and atmosphere of naturally occurring online communities, more evaluation is needed regarding the potential benefits and risks of using such widely used SNSs for this purpose.

In their commentary on the future of peer-to-peer support on social media, Naslund et al identified several risks that should be considered in the design of any platform that enables peer-to-peer support. First, there are risks inherent with obtaining advice from nonexpert peers who may unwittingly pass on misleading or unreliable information. Although research shows that many users of online health forums are aware of the need to evaluate the accuracy of advice received and whether it applies to their own circumstances, it is not known whether young people with mental health concerns do so routinely. Second, similar to all online environments, there is the potential to be exposed to hostile or derogatory comments from others, which could have a negative impact on the mental health of users. These key risks can be largely mitigated against on closed SNSs by having clinically trained moderators regularly review posts made by users so that they can clarify, correct, or potentially remove any posts that may be problematic for other users. Although none of the studies in this review reported the need to address any problematic posts, the MOST and YBMen interventions did have this ability, as their expert moderators were actively engaged with all content posted. The presence of expert moderators greatly contributed to users' perception of safety of the platforms.

[…]

Conclusions and Implications for Future Research

This review updates and expands previous reviews of the use of SNS for supporting youth mental health, which have, to date, only focused on specific disorders. By broadening the scope to include all aspects of mental health, including mental health literacy, this review shows that SNSs may play a useful role in providing mental health support to both clinical and nonclinical populations. It has also highlighted the importance of involving end users across all stages of intervention and platform design development according to participatory design principles and suggests that users prefer to be able to access SNS interventions on their mobile devices.

The evidence reviewed suggests that young people find SNS-based interventions highly usable, engaging, and supportive. However, high-quality evidence for their efficacy in reducing mental health symptoms is currently lacking. Furthermore, the majority of data collected in the reviewed studies came from participants aged over 18 years; therefore, there is a particular need for further investigation into the suitability of SNS-based interventions for adolescents aged less than 18 years. Now that proof-of-concept is established for some of the SNS interventions reviewed here, higher quality studies are required (ie, randomized controlled trials over longer periods), with populations that focus on adolescents as well as young adults, to build the evidence base in this field and address the following unanswered questions: Which aspects of SNS interventions are most beneficial for users and how do they mediate mental health outcomes?, Do skills gained online translate to sustained improvements in offline functioning and well-being?, Are some mental health issues and/or phases of the users' journey better suited to SNS interventions than others?, What level of participation is required from users to gain benefit?, Are mobile apps and mobile-friendly interfaces more beneficial for users?, and Is there an optimum user group/community size? There are also methodological challenges to address such as those associated with evaluating multicomponent interventions, collecting objective measures of mental health outcomes online, and dealing with variable levels of engagement and retention over longer periods.

Overall, the evidence reviewed suggests that both clinical and nonclinical users found SNS-based interventions to be safe, engaging, supportive, and useful. When moderated, ideally by mental health professionals, the benefits of SNS-based interventions for youth mental health appear to outweigh any potential risks. Given that young people are already turning to SNSs to engage in knowledge seeking and peer-to-peer support, SNS-based youth mental health interventions present a promising opportunity to help address some of the barriers young people face in accessing qualified mental health support and information. They also provide an opportunity to combine the well-established benefits of peer-to-peer support with accessible and cost-effective online interventions.

Organizations to Contact

The editors have compiled the following list of organizations concerned with the issues debated in this book. The descriptions are derived from materials provided by the organizations. All have publications or information available for interested readers. This list was compiled on the date of publication of the present volume; the information provided here may change. Be aware that many organizations take several weeks or longer to respond to inquiries, so allow as much time as possible.

Alcoholics Anonymous
475 Riverside Drive, 11th Floor
New York, NY 10115
phone: (212) 870-3400
email: info@aa-alive.org
website: www.aa.org

Established in 1935, Alcoholics Anonymous is a global network to support individuals working to maintain their sobriety. To join, members must have the desire to give up alcohol. Although it was founded in Akron, Ohio, Alcoholics Anonymous' headquarters are in New York.

American Academy of Child and Adolescent Psychiatry (AACAP)
3615 Wisconsin Avenue NW
Washington, DC 20016-3007
phone: (202) 966-7300
email: membership@aacap.org
websute www.aacap.org

The AACAP advocates for the healthy development of children, adolescents, and families. It supports and takes part in research, educational efforts, and policies with this goal in mind. It provides resources for both members and nonmembers of the organization.

American Foundation for Suicide Prevention
120 Wall Street, 29th Floor
New York, NY 10005
phone: (212) 363-3500
email: info@afsp.org
website: www.afsp.org

Started in 1987, the American Foundation for Suicide Prevention serves people whose lives have been affected by suicide. It funds scientific research on suicide, educates the public about suicide, and advocates for public policies related to mental health. Based in New York, it has chapters in fifty states and a public policy office in Washington, DC.

The American Institute of Stress
220 Adams Drive, Suite 280 , #224
Weatherford, TX 76086
phone: (682) 239-6823
email: info@stress.org
website: www.stress.org

The American Institute of Stress is a nonprofit corporation that began in 1978 in Yonkers, New York. Today, it is based in Texas. It works to give the public the tools needed to manage stressful situations and lead more fulfilling lives.

The Association of Black Psychologists
7119 Allentown Road, Suite 203
Ft. Washington, MD 20744
phone: (301) 449-3082
email: abpsi@abpsi.org
website: www.abpsi.org

The Association of Black Psychologists strives to meet the mental health needs of African Americans. It supports the practice of psychology with a distinctly black-African focus. It works to influence social change and provide black psychologists with a central organization through which they can champion black psychology.

Child Mind Institute
101 East 56th Street
New York, NY 10022
phone: (212) 308-3118
email: speakup@childmind.org
website: childmind.org

The Child Mind Institute is a nonprofit that serves children and families dealing with mental health and learning disorders. The institute strives to advance the research related to the developing brain. It also gives parents, professionals, and policymakers the tools needed to support children with mental health and learning problems.

National Alliance on Mental Illness
3803 N. Fairfax Drive, Suite 100
Arlington, VA 22203
phone: (703) 524-7600
email: info@nami.org
website: www.nami.org

The National Alliance on Mental Illness is a grassroots mental health organization focused on improving the lives of Americans grappling with mental health issues. It started in 1979 as a group of families meeting in a kitchen. Today, more than 500 local affiliates belong to the organization, which supports and educates people in need.

National Institute of Mental Health
Office of Science Policy, Planning, and Communications
6001 Executive Boulevard, Room 6200
MSC 9663
Bethesda, MD 20892-9663
phone: (866) 615-6464
email: nimhinfo@nih.gov
website: www.nimh.nih.gov

The National Institute of Mental Health is the federal government's top agency for research on mental disorders. It is one of the twenty-seven agencies that comprise the National Institutes of Health (NIH), the world's largest biomedical research agency in the world. NIH belongs to the US Department of Health and Human Services.

Substance Abuse and Mental Health Services
Administration (SAMHSA)
5600 Fishers Lane
Rockville, MD 20857
phone: (877) 726-4727
email: SAMHSAInfo@samhsa.hhs.gov
website: www.samhsa.gov

Established in 1992, SAMHSA is part of the US Department of Health and Human Services, the federal agency that works to improve the nation's behavioral health. SAMHSA leads the effort to reduce the effects of substance abuse and mental illness in the nation's communities.

Bibliography

Books

Joan Didion. *Blue Nights*. New York, NY: Knopf Doubleday, 2012.

Wayne Dyer. *10 Secrets for Success and Inner Peace*. Carlsbad, CA: Hay House, 2016.

Donna Freitas and Christian Smith. *The Happiness Effect: How Social Media Is Driving a Generation to Appear Perfect at Any Cost*. Oxford, UK: Oxford University Press, 2017.

Roxane Gay. *Hunger: A Memoir of (My) Body*. New York, NY: HarperCollins: 2017.

Stephen Grcevich. *Mental Health and the Church*. Grand Rapids, MI: Zondervan, 2018.

Julia F. Hastings, Lani V. Jones, and Pamela P. Martin. *African Americans and Depression*. Lanham, MD: Rowman & Littlefield Publishers, Inc., 2015.

Jon Kabat-Zinn. *Mindfulness for All: The Wisdom to Transform the World*. New York, NY: Hachette Books, 2019.

Autumn Libal. *Dissociative Disorders: The State of Mental Illness and its Therapy*. New York, NY: Simon & Schuster, 2014.

Natalia M. Lue. *The No Contact Rule*. Scotts Valley, CA: CreateSpace Publishing, 2013.

Jeff Mapua. *Coping With Cyberbullying*. New York, NY: Rosen Publishing Group, Inc., 2017.

Joyce Meyer. *Healing the Soul of a Woman: How to Overcome Your Emotional Wounds*. Nashville, TN: FaithWords, 2018.

Michael Noakes. *The Little Book of Self-Care*. London, UK: Ebury Press, 2017.

Peggy J. Parks. *Teens and PTSD*. San Diego, CA: Referencepoint Press, 2017.

Jill Savege Scharff. *Psychoanalysis Online: Mental Health, Teletherapy, and Training*. New York, NY: Routledge, 2018.

Ellen Greene Stewart. *Mental Health in Rural America: A Field Guide*. New York, NY: Routledge, 2018.

Rick Warren. *The Purpose Driven Life: What on Earth Am I Here For?* Grand Rapids, MI: Zondervan, 2013.

Elizabeth Wurtzel. *Prozac Nation: Young and Depressed in America*. Boston, MA: Houghton Mifflin Harcourt, 1994.

Periodicals and Internet Sources

Leonardo Blair, "Kay Warren Says Suicide Doesn't Condemn Believers," ChristianPost.com, September 10, 2015, https://www.christianpost.com/news/kay-warren-says-suicide-doesnt-condemn-believers-to-hell-says-she-prayed-audacious-prayers-before-son-took-his-life-145019/.

Adam Brady, "How Practicing Self-Care Can Improve Every Aspect of Your Life," The Chopra Center, retrieved May 28, 2019, https://chopra.com/articles/self-care-ideas-to-improve-your-life.

Leah Fessler, "The Hidden Emotional Consequences of De-friending Ex-pals and Former Flames," *Quartz*, March 1, 2017, https://qz.com/917100/think-defriending-people-will-make-you-feel-better-think-again/.

Olga Khazan, "Not White, Not Rich, and Seeking Therapy," *Atlantic*, June 1, 2016, https://www.theatlantic.com/health/archive/2016/06/the-struggle-of-seeking-therapy-while-poor/484970/.

Samantha Lauriello, "The Real Reason Record Numbers of College Students Are Seeking Mental Health Treatment," *Health*, January 25, 2019, https://www.health

.com/condition/depression/anxiety-depression-college
-university-students.

Jennifer Matesa, "Is Joan Didion in Denial About Her
Daughter's Alcoholism?" the *Fix*, December 8, 2011, https://
www.thefix.com/content/Joan-didion-quintana-roo
-blue%20nights-pancreatitis7033.

Brian Resnick, "Have Smartphones Really Destroyed a
Generation? We Don't Know," *Vox.co*, May 16, 2019, https://
www.vox.com/science-and-health/2019/2/20/18210498
/smartphones-tech-social-media-teens-depression-anxiety
-research.

Debbie Weingarten, "Why Are America's Farmers Killing
Themselves?" *Guardian*, December 6, 2017, https://www
.theguardian.com/us-news/2017/dec/06/why-are-americas
-farmers-killing-themselves-in-record-numbers.

A. J. Willingham and Elizabeth Elkin, "There's a Severe Shortage
of Mental Health Professionals in Rural Areas. Here's Why
That's a Serious Problem," CNN.com, June 22, 2018, https://
www.cnn.com/2018/06/20/health/mental-health-rural
-areas-issues-trnd/index.html.

Elizabeth Wurtzel, "Neither of My Parents Was Exactly Who I
Thought They Were," the *Cut*, December 26, 2018, https://
www.thecut.com/2018/12/elizabeth-wurtzel-on
-discovering-the-truth-about-her-parents.html.

Index